Wainwrig… northern England

A … Coast

Route Guide

Tony & Chris Grogan

SKYWARE PRESS 2014

St. Bees Head to Robin Hood's Bay

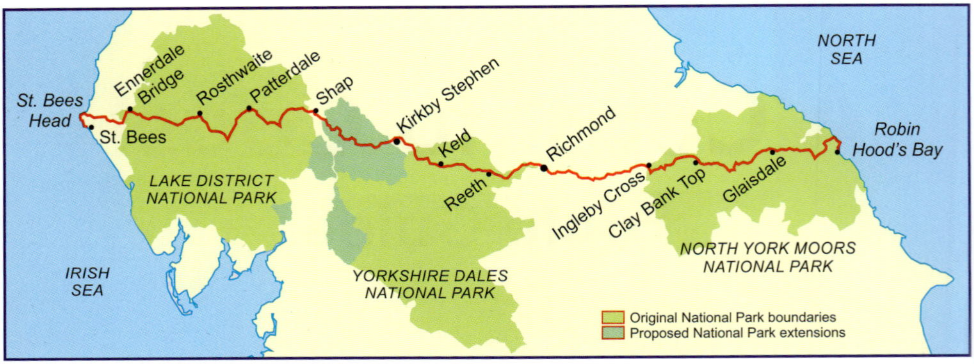

Wainwright's *Coast to Coast Walk* is by far the most popular long distance trail in Britain, and one of the world's great walks.

From the Irish Sea at St. Bees Head, it winds its way across northern England, 190 miles or so, to the North Sea shoreline at Robin Hood's Bay. On the way it passes through three national parks: the Lake District, the Yorkshire Dales and the North York Moors.

Almost everywhere the landscape is varied, full of interest and beauty. From seaside cliff tops the trail crosses high mountains and lakesides, heather moors and deep cut valleys, green rolling hills and gentle river tracks, calling at charming villages and towns along the way.

It is an exhilarating adventure, which once completed is an achievement that will remain fondly in the memory for the rest of your life.

This book is not designed as a replacement for Wainwright's original guidebook, but rather to complement it, to make the practical task of route-finding easier.

The Coast to Coast is a tough and challenging walk; even forewarned many people still find it tougher than they expected, particularly over Lakeland. The key to success is careful preparation.

Wainwright divided his walk into 12 sections, and this route guide follows suit. Strong and experienced fell walkers may tackle one section a day, but for most walkers some sections are just too long. It's better to break them and take time to explore. 14 or 15 days make better itineraries, whilst still allowing the walk to fit into a fortnight slot. Popular break points include Black Sail Hut or Honister on section 2; Grasmere on section 3; Orton or Newbiggin-on-Lune on section 5; Catterick Bridge or Danby Wiske on section 9; Blakey Ridge on section 11; and Grosmont or Hawsker on section 12.

Most guidebooks follow Wainwright's lead and give the distance of the Coast to Coast path as 190 miles (306 km). The route here measured by digital mapping software gives a figure of about 185 miles (298 km), but this tends to smooth out the route and experience shows that this underestimates real walking on the ground by around 5%. So you should expect to walk *at least* between 190 and 200 miles (322 km) to complete the walk.

The main route shown is the modern route as currently promoted by the Wainwright Society – the body responsible for looking after the Coast to Coast Walk. Wainwright's alternative sections are also shown, as are some popular alternatives promoted by other authors. Where the route has changed significantly, the original route is also shown, where it is currently accessible. This is both for historical interest and for the benefit of walkers who have older guidebooks.

The strip maps in this guide are aligned in the general direction of travel, which varies from map to map. The maps are based on OS Explorer maps at a scale of 1:25,000, but with superfluous detail omitted and with some features exaggerated for clarity. The route has been surveyed on the ground prior to publication, but bear in mind that the countryside changes – new fences appear, signs disappear, stiles are replaced by gates.

The appropriate OS Explorer maps at 1:25,000 are useful for getting a wider picture, for diversions, or if you get lost. The most useful are those covering the national parks: OL4 and OL5 for the Lakes; OL19 and OL30 for the Yorkshire Dales; and OL26 and OL27 for the North York Moors.

As the photos in this book show, the sun always shines on Coast to Coast walkers – but only the very lucky ones. Most people will get rained on some of the time; some people will get rained on most of the time. So carry a set of waterproofs alongside the sun block, plenty of water and enough food for a full day.

A compass or GPS is absolutely essential for misty conditions, and a mobile phone can be useful in emergencies – although you may not always get a signal. If you get into trouble on the fells, at the first opportunity call 999 and ask for the POLICE, then tell them you need MOUNTAIN RESCUE. Information about any route changes, accommodation, other resources, etc. can be found on the associated website at ***www.coastto.co.uk***

As Wainwright wrote, you are free to vary the route as you see fit, so long as this doesn't involve trespass, and to take shortcuts where necessary. Dispel any notion that this is somehow cheating: *The way you go and the time it takes matter not. The essence of the walk is the crossing of England, from one coast to the other, on foot*

A brief history of the Coast to Coast Walk

Sometime in the late 1960s Alfred Wainwright laid a ruler across a map of northern England, and drew a pencil line from St Bees Head to Robin Hood's Bay. With that stroke of genius he created one of the world's great walks.

Wainwright had risen to fame with the publication of his *Pictorial Guides to the Lakeland Fells* (1955–1966), which he created in his spare time whilst working as the borough treasurer at Kendal.

Wainwright walked the Pennine Way soon after it was opened as Britain's first national trail and his *Pennine Way Companion* was published in 1968, but it was not a walk he enjoyed and it set him thinking of his own *superior* and *unofficial* long-distance trail.

Wainwright began to flesh out the detail of his Coast to Coast Walk in early 1970, starting with the North York Moors where he'd never been before. It was the happiest of times for Wainwright – he was now retired and could devote his attention full time to his walks, and in March he'd married his second wife Betty.

Whilst honeymooning in York Wainwright first visited the Cleveland Hills, looking to devise a route along the Cleveland Way and Lyke Wake Walk. For Wainwright the Cleveland escarpment proved one of the highlights of the whole walk outside Lakeland.

Next he turned his attention to the Yorkshire Dales. He toyed with the idea of using the newly created Dales Way as a route into Yorkshire, whilst working on *Walks on the Howgill Fells* (published in 1972). In the end he opted for a more northerly route across the Westmorland Fells to Kirkby Stephen, then across the Pennine watershed into Swaledale. The lead mines of Swaledale proved another highlight for Wainwright.

Finally Wainwright worked a route across his cherished Lakeland Fells.

He finished his *Coast to Coast Walk* in early 1972 and it was published the following year by the Westmorland Gazette. Wainwright sat back and waited. At first he was surprised at the apparent lack of response. He received hundreds of letters each year from walkers finishing the Pennine Way, but by spring 1974 he had received only two letters from walkers completing the Coast to Coast.

Wainwright need not have worried – the walk quickly grew to become the most popular long-distance trail in Britain.

Wainwright revisited the walk for BBC television in 1989, aged 82, in the company of broadcaster Eric Robson. The four part series presented a gentle and affectionate account of the walk, and it is clear from the film that Wainwright was proud of his creation. Wainwright died two years later and in keeping with his wishes, his ashes were scattered at Innominate Tarn on Haystacks, overlooking his Coast to Coast Walk.

Route Changes

Since Wainwright's *Coast to Coast Walk* was first published in 1973 there have been a number of changes to the route.

Despite Wainwright's intention *to use only rights of way and areas of open access*, his route in places followed tracks across private land that were not rights of way. This became a particular problem in the section between Shap and Kirkby Stephen. The local authorities were later able to negotiate

Alfred Wainwright and Betty at the Dalesman offices, Clapham 1987

permissive status with land owners on some tracks which allowed their continued use. In other places this was not possible.

In 1981 the route across Great Asby Scar was diverted along the road into Orton and then on through Raisbeck to Sunbiggin Tarn. The modern route which skirts to the north of Orton was introduced in the first revised edition in 1994, after Wainwright's death.

The route around Sunbiggin Tarn had to be diverted for similar reasons, initially to follow roads to the north. In 2003 the county council created a new public right of way across Ravenstonedale Moor to the south of Sunbiggin Tarn, and this became the basis for the modern route.

Ironically, by this time the passing of the Countryside and Rights of Way Act 2000 meant that much of Wainwright's original route became publically accessible under the new *right to roam* legislation. Perhaps Wainwright was just ahead of his time.

Elsewhere Wainwright's route problems were of an entirely different nature. Many of the rights of way across the Vale of Mowbray were neglected and inaccessible. Wainwright found himself *beaten back to the tarmac by barbed wire, dykes, too-friendly bovines and other obstacles.* He was forced to revert to quiet country roads for over eight miles. Today things are much improved, and the modern route now follows easily along grassy footpaths for most of this section, just as Wainwright originally intended.

The popularity of the walk created problems over the wet, peaty moors at Nine Standards Rigg. Wainwright's original route followed a bridleway up to Rollinson Haggs, but erosion led to the ascent being diverted to the more direct and firmer going alongside Faraday Gill in 1992. At the same time the route along the ridge was diverted to head east, straight down across the moors to join Whitsundale Beck (the modern BLUE route). This route proved just as susceptible to erosion as the original, so in 1998 the modern seasonal three-route system was introduced.

The Coast to Coast today

Soon after Wainwright's death Michael Joseph took over the publication of his books, and the first guidebooks written by other authors began to appear, including those by Paul Hannon (Hillside 1992) and Terry Marsh (Cicerone 1993). Both authors brought a fresh outlook to the problems facing the trail, and some of their alternatives have since been incorporated into the modern route. Other guidebooks followed, including Henry Stedman (Trailblazer 2004), Martin Wainwright (Aurum 2007) and Sandra Bardwell (Rucksack Readers 2010). Strip maps also appeared, including the popular Ordnance Survey maps at 1:25,000 (now discontinued), Harvey maps at 1:40,000 and Footprint maps at 1:50,000.

In 2003 Michael Joseph (now part of the Penguin group) ceased printing Wainwright's guides, saying they were no longer in demand. Francis Lincoln took over.

The Coast to Coast was given another boost in 2009 when Julia Bradbury presented her own account of the walk in a six-part television series, filmed under typically wet Coast to Coast conditions.

In 2010 a brand new "second edition" of Wainwright's *Coast to Coast Walk*, revised by Chris Jesty, was published by Francis Lincoln, incorporating all the route changes that had taken place.

The Wainwright Society now took on responsibility for the Coast to Coast Walk. The society was founded in 2002 with its primary aim being to keep alive the fellwalking traditions promoted by Alfred Wainwright through his guidebooks and other publications.

At its annual meeting in 2012, chairman Eric Robson announced that the walk would be waymarked for the first time in 40 years. The Society undertook negotiations with all the local authorities along the way, to iron out any remaining difficulties and fix a modern definitive route.

Section 1: **St. Bees to Ennerdale Bridge**

14.3 miles (*23.0 km*)

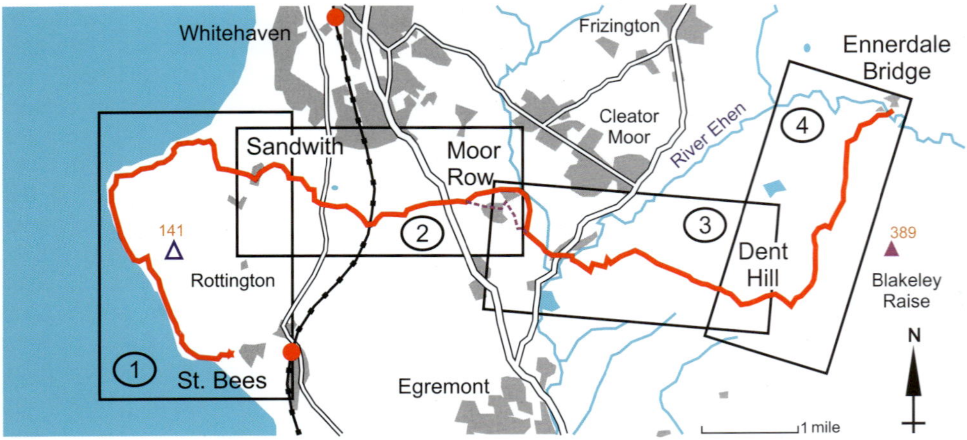

It's hard to imagine a better start to your journey. The day begins with a lofty stroll along the cliff edges of St. Bees Head, and finishes with your first close tantalising views of the mountains of Wainwright's beloved Lakeland.

At around 14½ miles this makes a good first day's walk, if you get an early enough start.

Its long sandy beach has made St. Bees a popular holiday destination, with plenty of accommodation and facilities, though there's a three-quarter mile walk first from the village to the shore.

The walk starts at the sea wall, approached from the village of St. Bees along Beach Road.

Locate the Coast to Coast information board and, if the tide is in, dip your boots in the Irish Sea before setting off northwest to cross Rottington Beck and climb up following the cliff edge. No problems with route finding here, though coastal erosion is pushing the path inside the fence.

A fine lofty walk above the red sandstone cliffs of South Head brings you quickly to Fleswick Bay, before another climb around the North Head.

The Isle of Man can be seen westward, with the Scottish lowland hills of the Galloway coast to the north.

The coast is finally left just beyond a disused quarry, following the road into Sandwith.

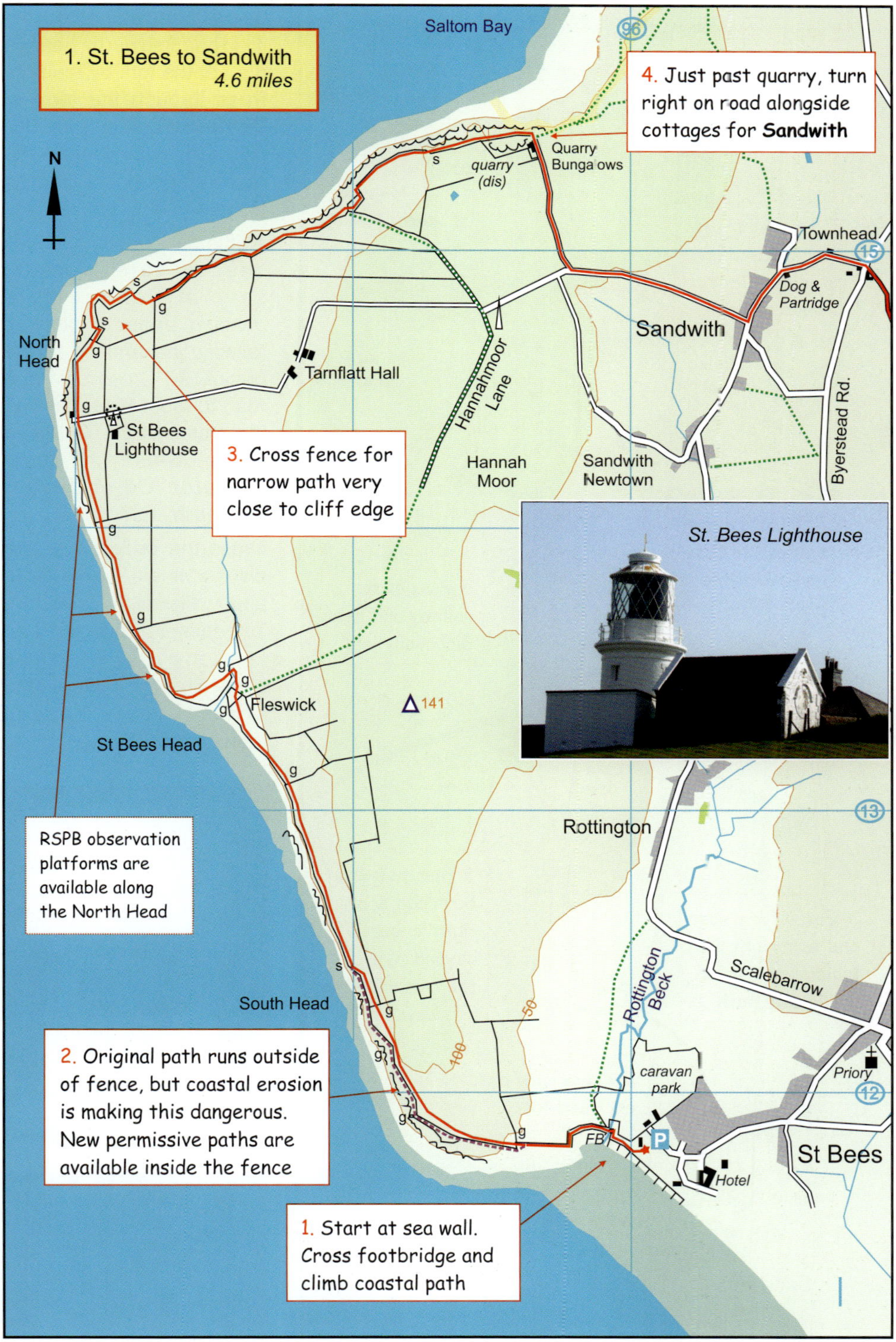
1. St. Bees to Sandwith
4.6 miles
Saltom Bay
N
96
4. Just past quarry, turn right on road alongside cottages for **Sandwith**
Quarry Bungalows
quarry (dis)
s
Townhead
15
Dog & Partridge
Sandwith
Hannahmoor Lane
Tarnflatt Hall
North Head
St Bees Lighthouse
3. Cross fence for narrow path very close to cliff edge
Hannah Moor
Sandwith Newtown
Byerstead Rd.
St. Bees Lighthouse
Fleswick
141
St Bees Head
Rottington
13
RSPB observation platforms are available along the North Head
Scalebarrow
Rottington Beck
South Head
50
100
caravan park
Priory
12
2. Original path runs outside of fence, but coastal erosion is making this dangerous. New permissive paths are available inside the fence
FB
P
Hotel
St Bees
1. Start at sea wall. Cross footbridge and climb coastal path

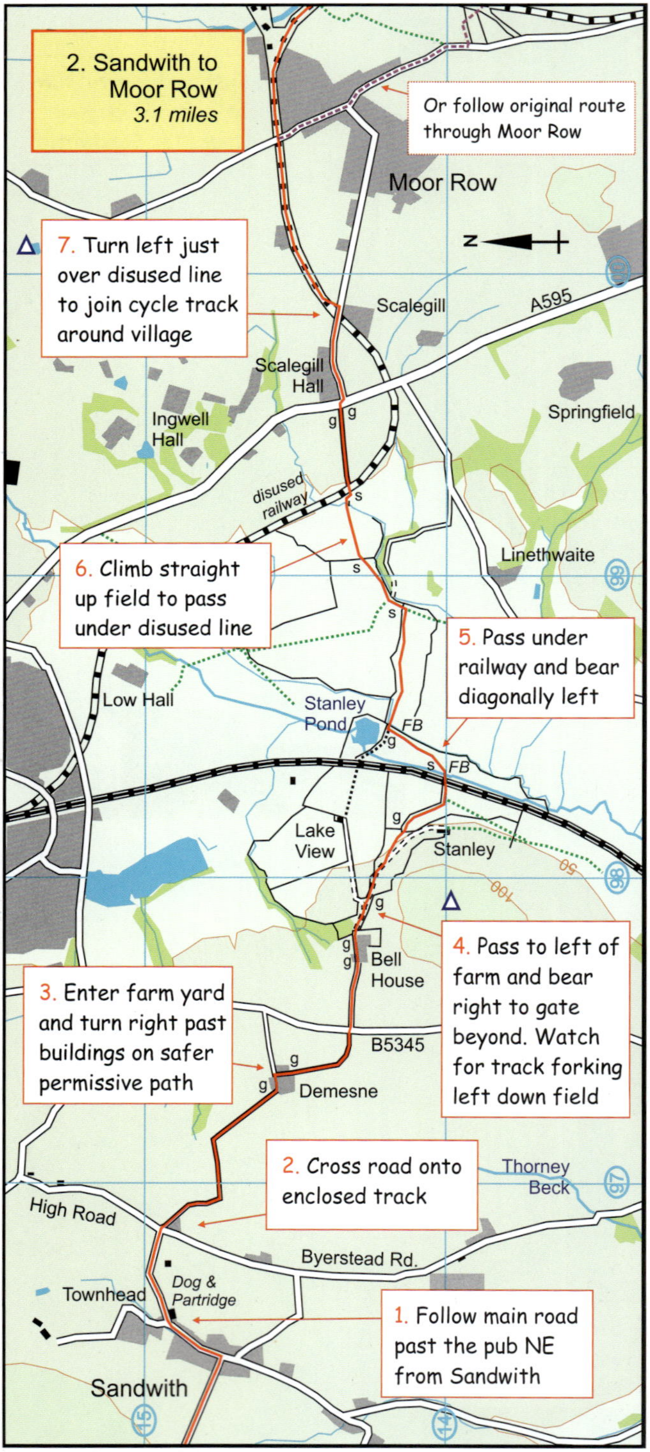

Leave Sandwith along the road heading north, bearing right at the fork by the pub. Pass through the farm at **Demesne** and on past Bell House, to pass beneath the railway and on to Stanley Pond.

A little careful navigation is needed here crossing several fields before passing under a disused railway line and up to the busy A595. Cross to join the road to Moor Row, passing the statue of the ***Coast to Coast*** walker by local sculptor Colin Telfer, erected in 2007.

Cross the bridge over the disused line – now a cycle and walkway - and turn immediately left to join it on the modern route bypassing the village (the original route passes through Moor Row).

Just past Moor Row, at a fork in the cycleway path go right, then left along **Hadrian's Cycleway**. After a further half mile leave the tarmac path and cut down on a rough parallel track to the left (easily missed) to join an enclosed way, leading down to Cleator.

Like Moor Row before it, Cleator shows the influence of the 19th century iron ore mining industry in rows of tiny cramped terraced cottages built for the influx of migrant workers in the boom years. Leave the main street on a road opposite the local store, turn right onto a road signed **Miller's Walk** to cross Blackhow Bridge. Head up to Blackhow Farm and cross the road onto a forest track. This climbs steeply. Watch out for a footpath sign for **Dent Fell** on the left, which leads you onto a shady forest path heading steeply uphill. Finally on the summit of Dent Hill the first sight of the nearby Lakeland Fells is a moment to relish.

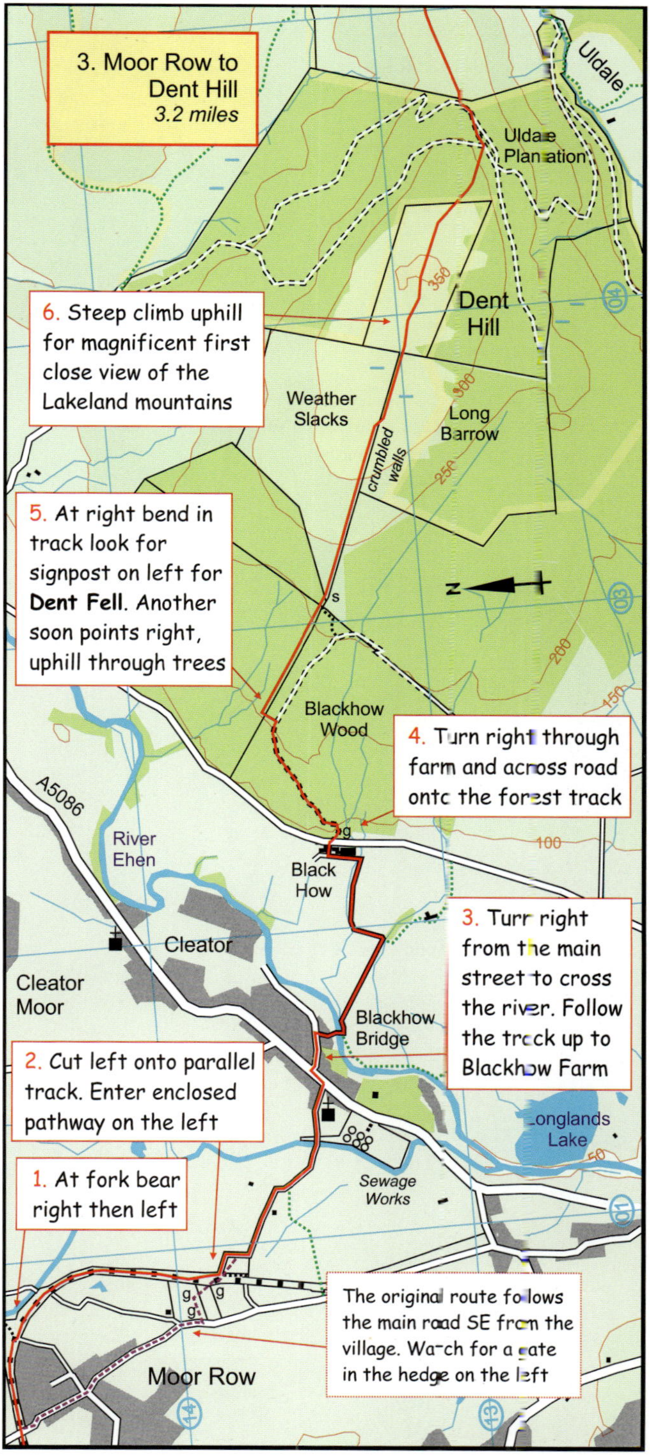

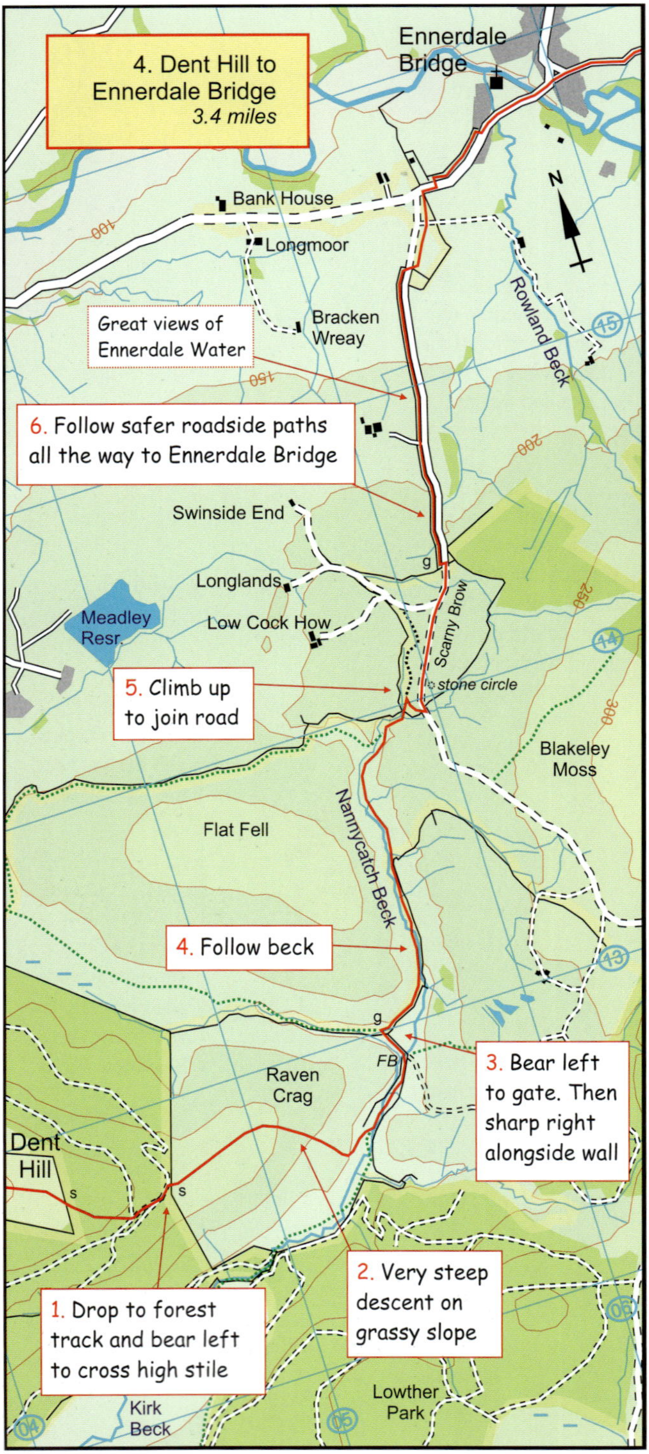

From the top of Dent Hill the track leads down towards some trees and a forest track, where a left turn brings you to a very high ladder stile. The grassy path then drops very steeply over Raven Crag down to the lovely Nannycatch Beck.

The walk along the quiet beckside is a sheer delight.

Finally the path climbs up to join the road into Ennerdale Bridge. Just over the road, a seemingly prehistoric stone circle is actually a 20th century creation.

Follow the road on the verges, taking to roadside walkers' paths installed by the local parish council beyond the cattle grid. At peak times the fast traffic to and from Sellafield makes the narrow road quite dangerous.

A glimpse of Ennerdale Water comes into view, with the high mountians of Great Borne, Starling Dodd, Red Pike and High Stile acting as a dramatic backdrop.

Looking back along the ridge from High Stile to Red Pike, with Bleaberry Tarn and Crummack Water (top).

The lonely Black Sail Hut, Ennerdale (right).

Innominate Tarn, Haystacks, Wainwright's final resting place (bottom).

Section 2: **Ennerdale Bridge to Rosthwaite**

14.7 miles (23.7 km)

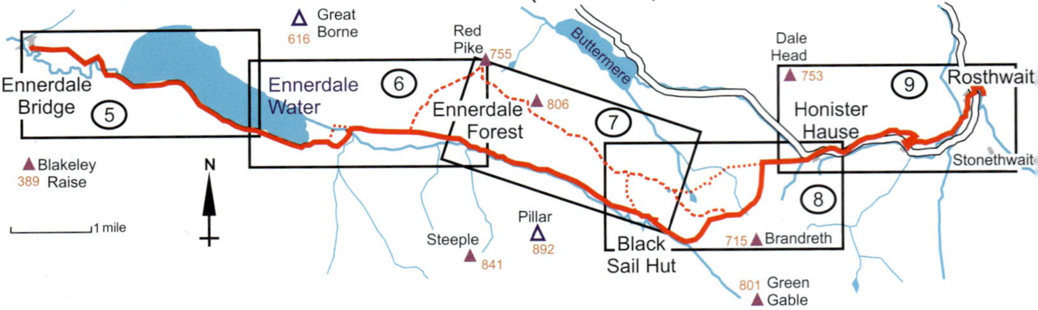

An exciting day ahead as you plunge into Lakeland proper. At a little under 15 miles it's quite a long section, but a string of youth hostels offer opportunities to break it. The most romantic is Black Sail Hut but Honister is also a popular choice.

The section begins with a pleasant lakeside ramble leading to a long but easy forest trail. Then the first real climb of the journey up Loft Beck, where care is required in bad weather; not an unlikely prospect - you're heading into the wettest region in England!

Wainwright offers the option of a high level alternative along the High Stile ridge; stunning but tough going. Think carefully before taking this on so early into the walk.

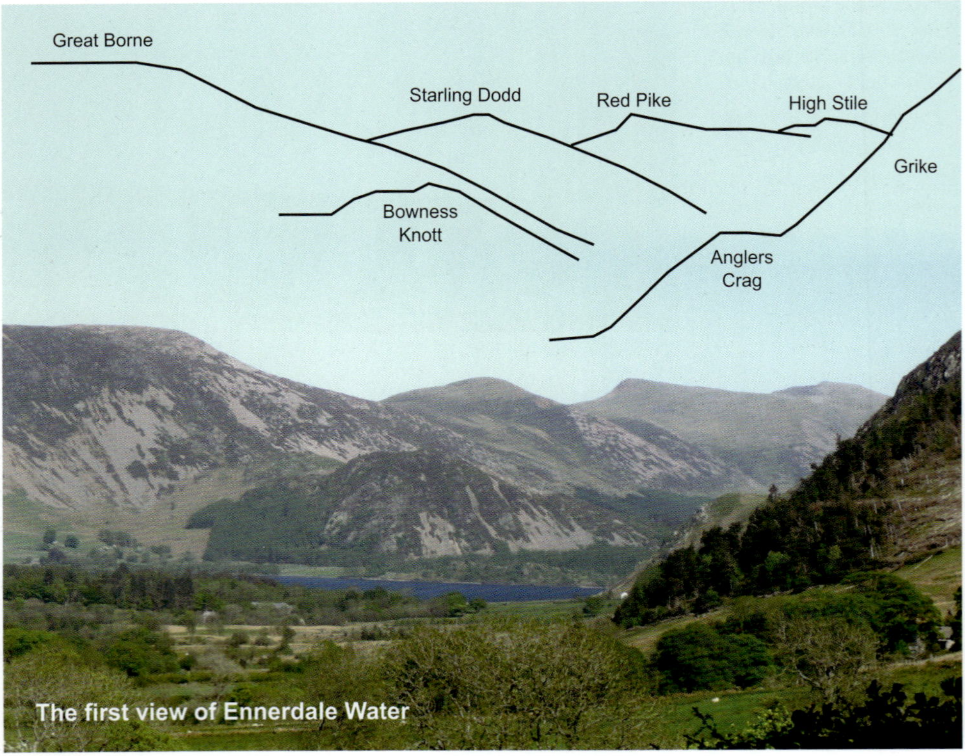

The first view of Ennerdale Water

Leave Ennerdale Bridge on the Croasdale Road heading east. Take the right fork which zigzags down to the lake and pick up the path along the southern shore.

The path along the south side of Ennerdale Water is rough and rocky and often wet, so it's sometimes hard to lift your eyes.

Beneath Anglers Crag a tricky little climb over the steep-sided rockface is necessary. Route finding though is easy.

Another option in bad weather is to take the path along the northern shore, which is easier underfoot and soon becomes a clear forest track. Though slightly longer it is in fact quicker.

Ennerdale Water is the most westerly and remote of the lakes and consequently the most unspoilt. At 2½ miles long, ¾ mile wide and 45 metres deep, it acts as a reservoir with its clear waters serving the coastal towns of Cumbria.

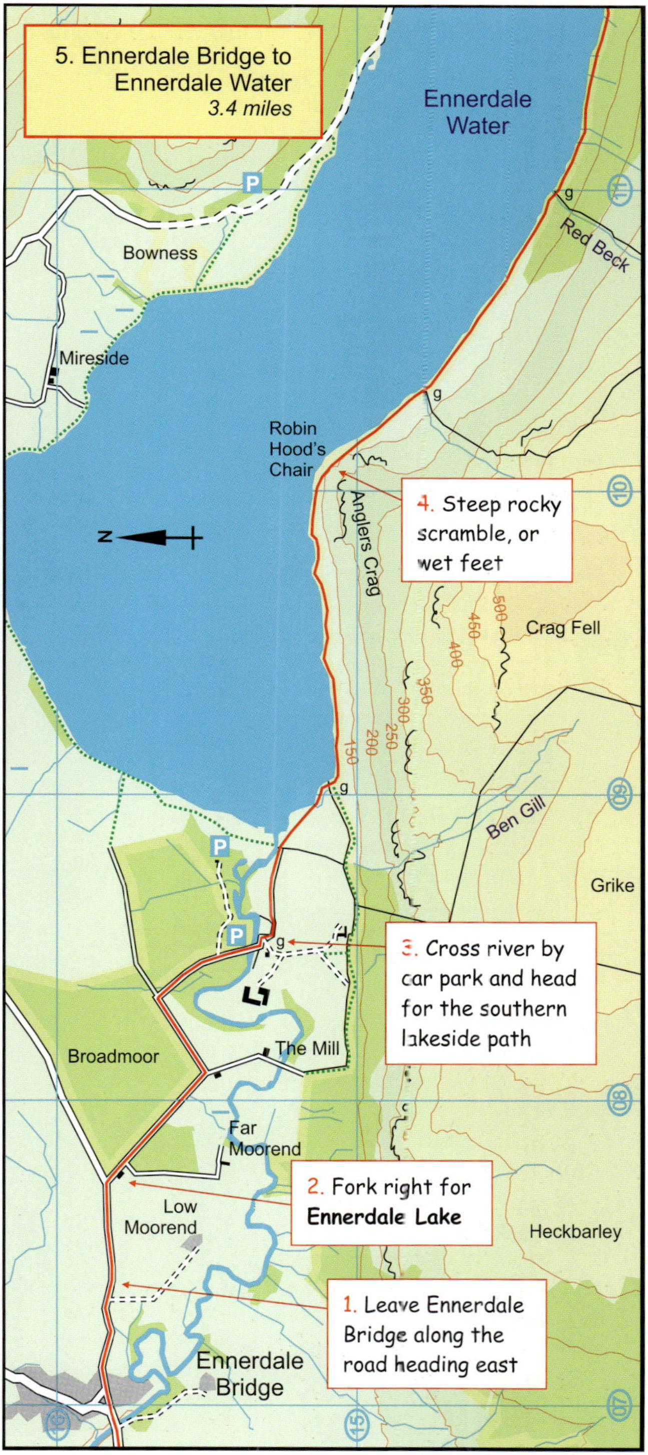

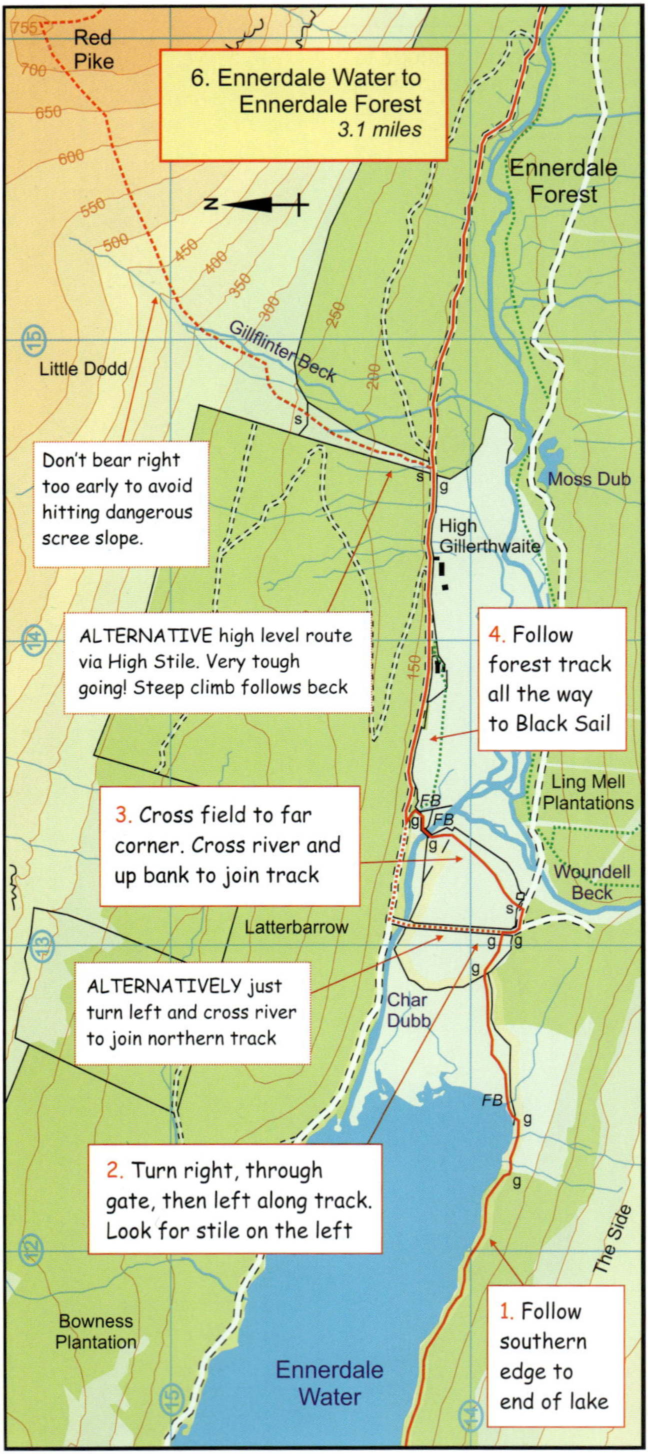

Beyond the end of the lake the Coast to Coast path crosses to the forest track on the northern side of the river, though the track and footpath on the southern side can be followed just as easily.

It is easy walking now all the way to the top of the valley and the lonely youth hostel at Black Sail Hut.

Just beyond High Gillerthwaite there's the option of a tough high level alternative, for experienced fell walkers on a clear day only. A stile on the left leads to a very steep track rising alongside Gillflinter Beck, before veering towards the summit of Red Pike. Don't veer too early though, as you may end up on dangerous scree. There follows a truly spectacular ridge walk to Haystacks (Wainwright's favourite mountain).

The forest is now much less oppressive than it once was for early walkers on the Coast to Coast. Planted after the first world war when there was a strategic need for a secure timber supply, the valley was filled with a densely packed monoculture of Sitka spruce. But times have changed, and when timber became less economical towards the end of the last century, the Forestry Commission began to develop a more progressive strategy to forest management.

Today Ennerdale is managed by a partnership of the main landowners – the Forestry Commission, National Trust, United Utilities and Natural England under the title ***Wild Ennerdale***, with a vision *to allow the evolution of Ennerdale as a wild valley for the benefit of people, relying more on natural processes to shape its landscape and ecology.*

The conifers are being thinned, and cleared altogether in areas where they are a particular visual detriment to the landscape. Native broadleaf species are being introduced.

Approaching Black Sail Hut

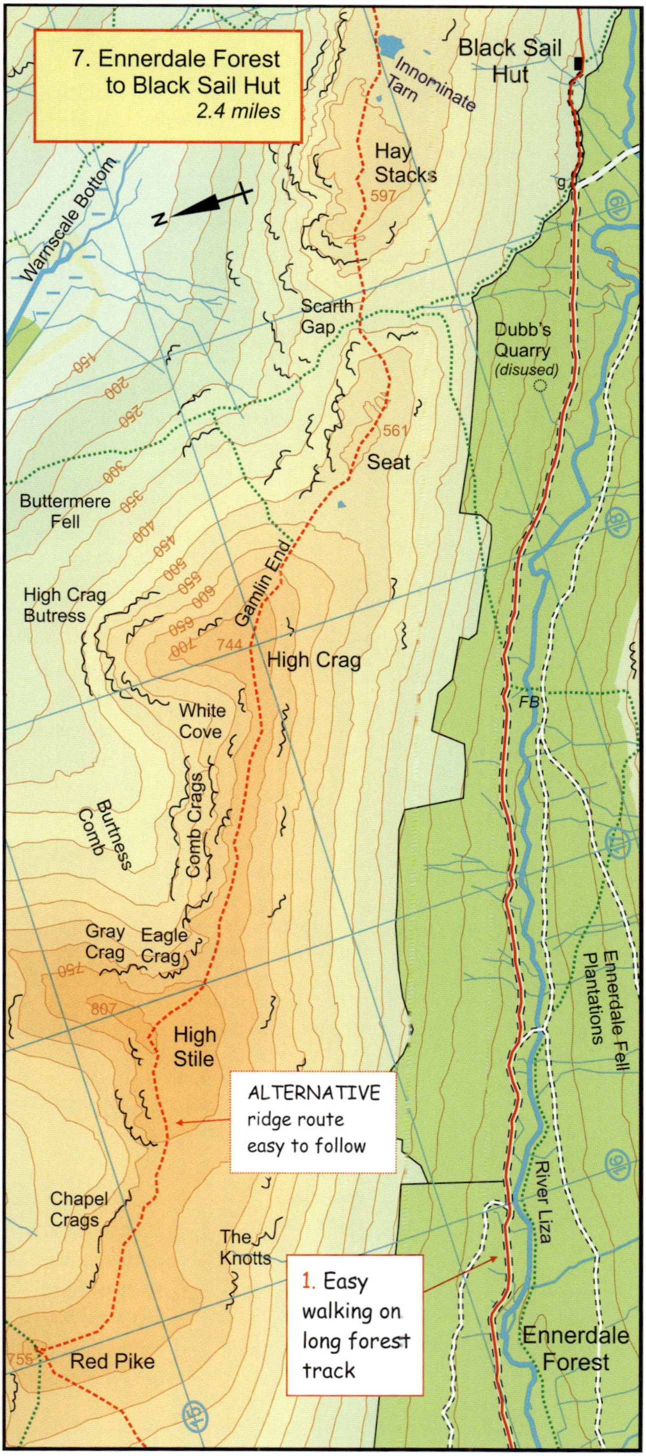

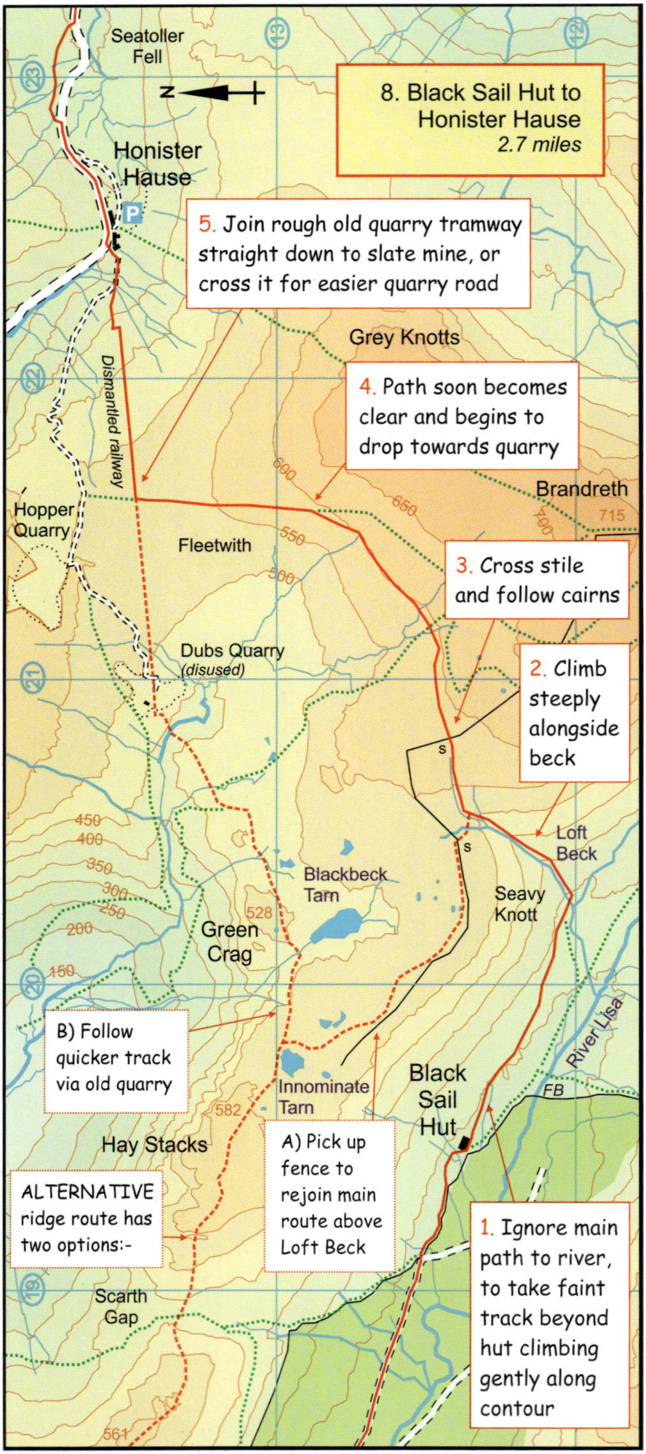

Don't leave Black Sail Hut along the main path heading SE to cross the river, but pick up a faint track beyond the hut that hugs the contour, becoming clearer as Loft Beck comes into view. The climb on the right of the beck is steep but clear.

Climbing Loft Beck into mist

As the top of Loft Beck approaches, the path crosses at a couple of points, before veering right to climb along the right side of a tributary stream, heading just north of east. Care is needed here in misty conditions, as the route is not clear. Cross the Brandreth fence at a stile and follow a line of cairns striding straight ahead eastwards, curving northeast and eventually meeting a more prominent track to begin descending northwards to join the disused quarry railway track which leads straight down to the slate mine visitor centre at Honister.

Visitor centre beneath Honister Crag

Slate mining and quarrying at Honister was first recorded in the early 18th century; by 1891 production had reached 3,000 tons a year and more than 100 men were employed. Honister Hause became the centre of operations - a former quarry workers' house is now the youth hostel here.

The slate mine almost closed for good in the late 1980s, until the present owners acquired it and reopened it as a working mine and popular tourist attraction.

The route down towards Borrowdale follows the busy pass road, making use of an old coach track which shadows it down to the tiny village of Seatoller.

A path from the back of the car park then skirts the edge of Johnny Wood for the youth hostel at Longthwaite. Leave here across the river bridge, bearing left to pass between houses for a footpath across fields and into Rosthwaite.

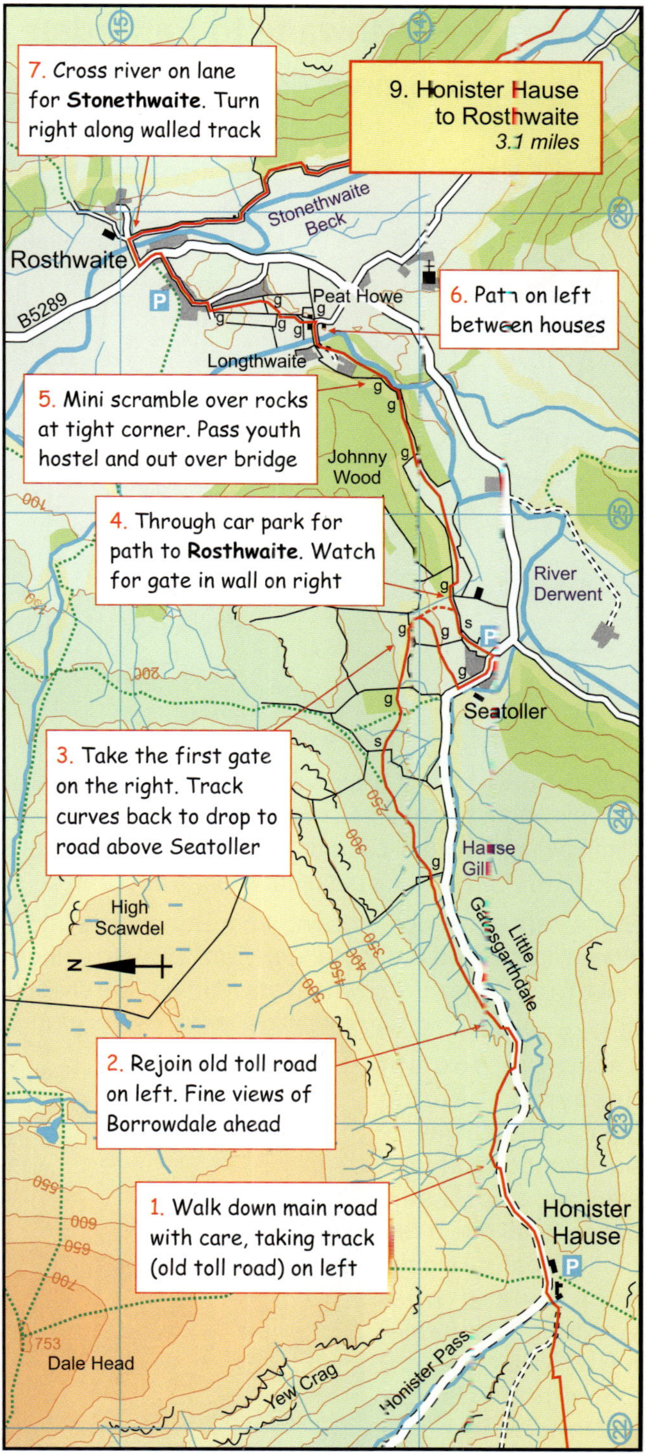

Section 3: **Rosthwaite to Patterdale**

15.5 miles (*24.9 km*)

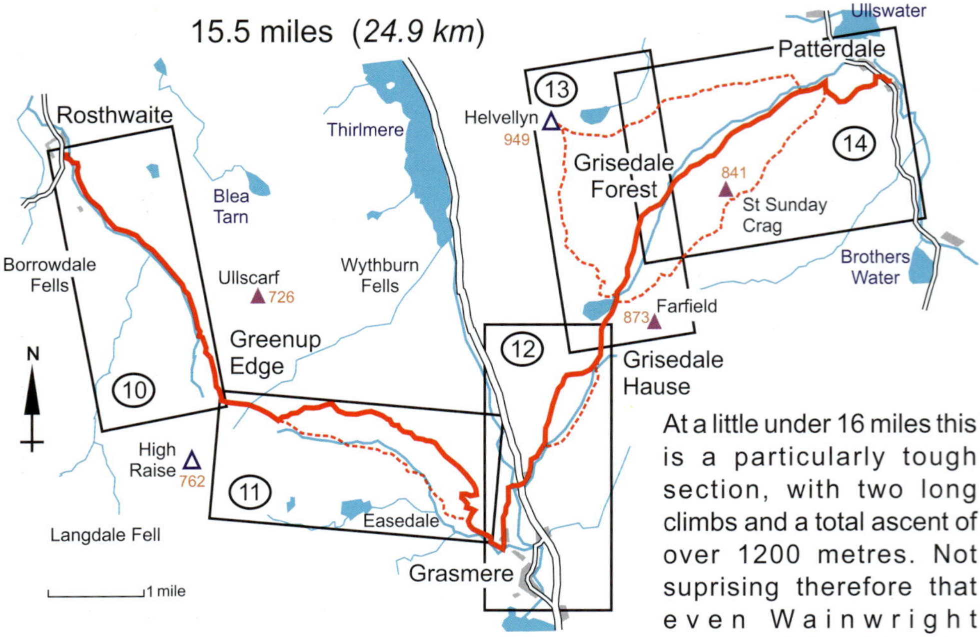

At a little under 16 miles this is a particularly tough section, with two long climbs and a total ascent of over 1200 metres. Not suprising therefore that even Wainwright suggested breaking this section at Grasmere, advice which most walkers are happy to take.

With two days at your disposal and good weather there's the opportunity to take one of Wainwright's suggested high level alternatives from Grisedale Hause: the lovely climb over St Sunday Crag or the terrifying traverse of Striding Edge. Otherwise the trek down Grisedale is a pleasant enough descent.

Some care is needed crossing from Borrowdale into Far Easedale, avoiding what Wainwright called the *Wythburn Trap*. The easy ridge walk to the modest peak of Helm Crag – one of Wainwright's favourites - is a sheer delight.

Grasmere is a veritable tourist honeypot, offering plenty in the way of accommodation and supplies, as well as the option to take in a few of the tourist sights, such as the poet Wordsworth's former home at Dove Cottage, with the adjoining museum.

Taking a break at Grisedale Head, with St Sunday Crag as backdrop

Leave Rosthwaite on the main road heading north towards Keswick. Turn right onto the lane for **Stonethwaite**, across the bridge and right on the enclosed track that follows the beck south.

Easy route finding now. Follow the beck upstream until it splits below the impressive Eagle Crag, where a footbridge below takes the Cumbria Way SW alongside Langstrath Beck for the Snake Pass into Langdale. Continue straight on to start the climb alongside the cascading waters of Greenup Gill and up to the rocky pinnacle of Lining Crag.

The climb to Lining Crag

Beyond Lining Crag the route again is tricky, even in clear weather, as you climb south over boggy ground, with no clear track. Eventually some rocky outcrops on the ridge ahead come into view. Keep to the right of a prominent outcrop with an old metal fencepost sticking up on top.

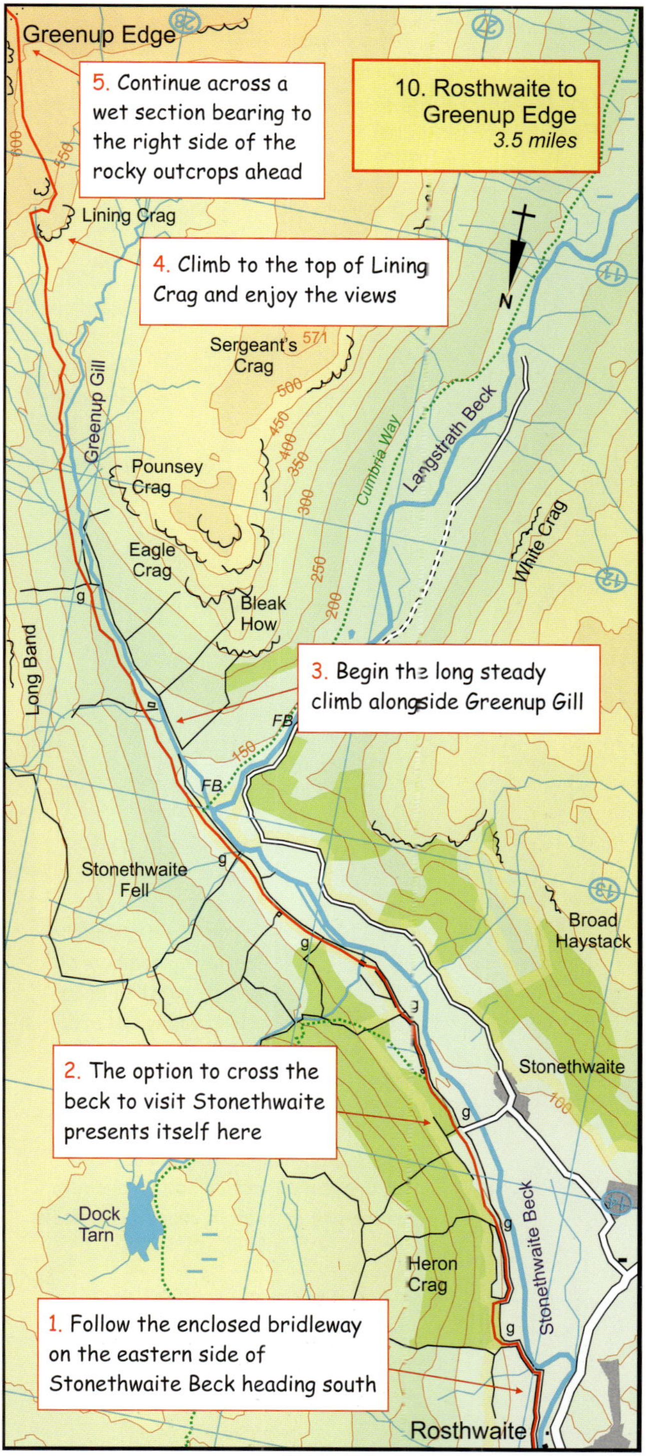

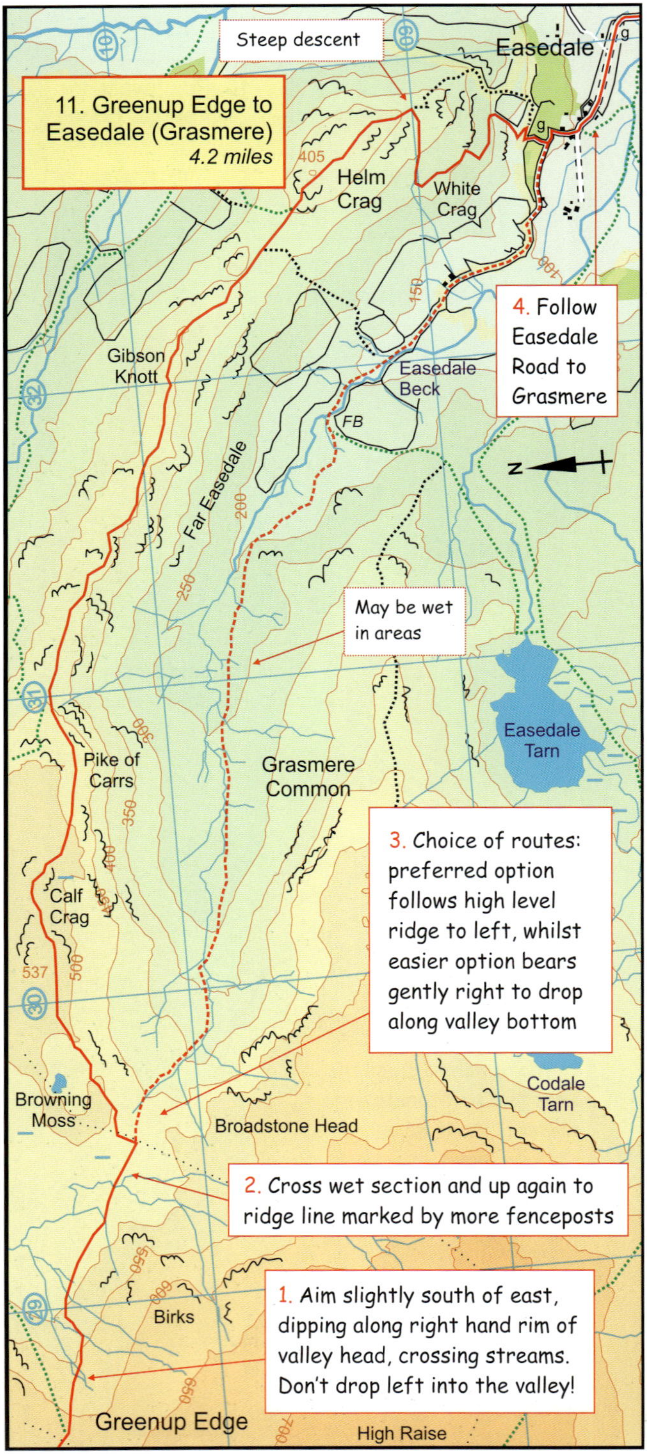

Once at the ridge, the head of the Wythburn Valley lies ahead. The aim is to bear just south of east across the valley's head, aiming for a dip in the ridge opposite (if it can be seen). There is a danger here of bearing north down into the valley following the streams – what Wainwright called the *Wythburn Trap*.

From the ridge the indistinct path cuts down to the right, to skirt around the rim of Wythburn Head, crossing streams as it first descends, then flattens on boggy ground, before gently rising to the ridge above Far Easedale, marked also with old metal fenceposts.

Here an option presents itself: follow the clear track bearing left for a fine ridge walk across Calf Crag, Pike of Carrs, Gibson Knott and Helm Crag - the preferred option; or if the weather is bad or time is pressing, bear right on the track down into the valley.

If the target is Grasmere, continue along the Easedale Road into the village, adding a half mile (both ways).

The Howitzer, Helm Crag

Alongside Stonethwaite Beck, approaching Greenup Gill, Borrowdale (above).

At the top of Great Tongue, looking back towards Grasmere (below).

Descending towards the knife-edge ridge of Striding Edge, Helvellyn (right).

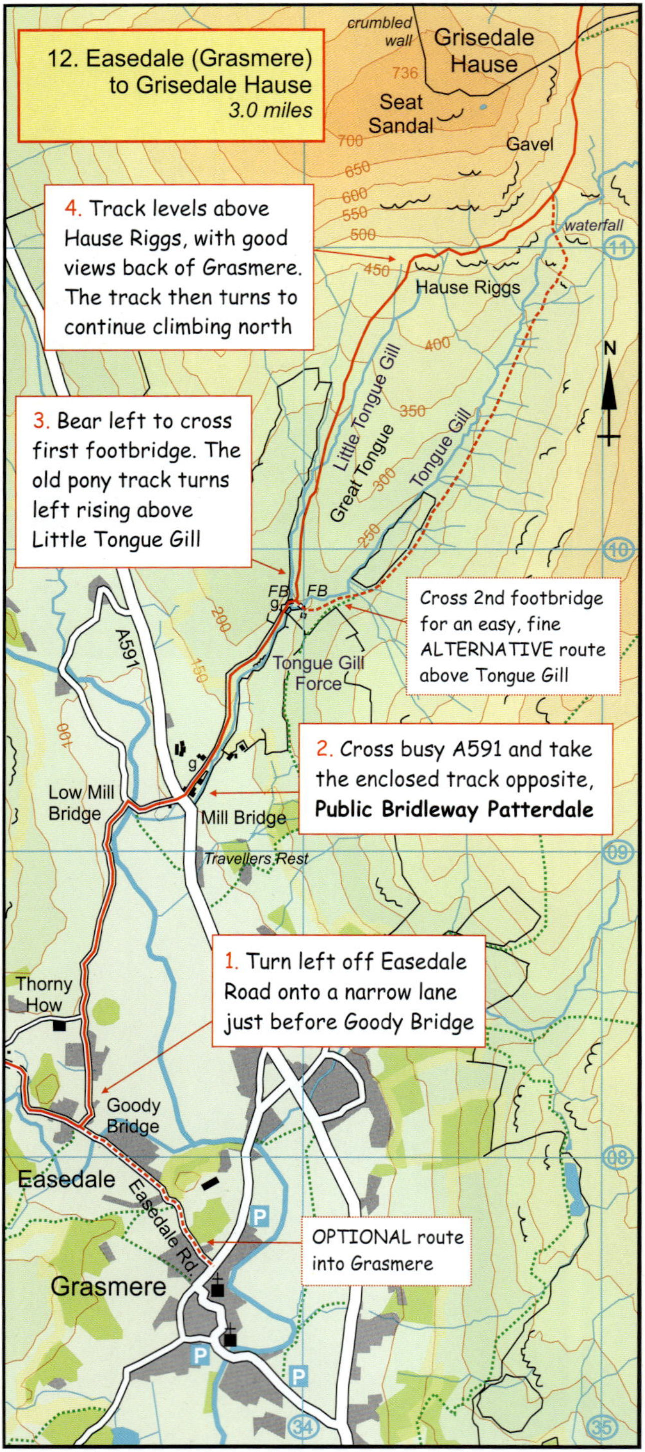

From Easedale Road take the lane north by Goody Bridge past Thorny How youth hostel, across the River Rawthey and on to the busy A591 at Mill Bridge. Cross and pick up the narrow bridleway track for **Patterdale**, which climbs quickly to a gate beneath Great Tongue.

Across the footbridge a choice of routes is available. The main route bears left up a steep grassy track, an old pony trail, alongside Little Tongue Gill. This is tough going at first, but rewarded with excellent views back to Grasmere. A more popular alternative crosses a second footbridge to climb alongside Tongue Gill on the east of Great Tongue. Though easier, it lacks the views of the former.

The two paths meet at Hause Moss and a further short climb brings you to the pass at Grisedale Hause, and the welcoming sight of Grisedale Tarn.

The main route to Patterdale is an easy, if long, rocky path down into the valley, to join a farm track following the south bank of Grisedale Beck. A field path eventually cuts off through Glenamara Park to come out again near the village store.

A tough, but exhilarating alternative is the climb up to *Helvellyn* and the crossing of the knife-edge ridge of

Striding Edge. This should only be attempted in clear weather by experienced fell walkers with nerves of steel, plenty of energy and a good head for heights.

From Grisedale Tarn the path zigzags steeply up to Dollywaggon Pike and then follows a long ridge walk up to the summit of Helvellyn. From here cut back SE past the shelter and Gough's memorial before a very tricky steep descent to the ridge. The first buttress can be climbed or skirted by a narrow path to the right, before the edge itself is tackled. A thin path just below the ridge top on the left makes going much easier. Beyond the edge the route is straightforward – on to the Hole-in-the-Wall for a steady descent into Grisedale.

The alternative route via St. Sunday Crag makes a really fine mountain trek, with the added attraction of almost guaranteed seclusion. A faint path rises gently from the NE edge of the tarn. Eventually a steep right turn brings you onto the ridge at Deepdale Hause and a left leads on up to the summit. Bear north from here. The path down is unclear in places, but curves gently down to the right, bearing NE, with magnificent views ahead of Ullswater all the way. A final steep descent to Glenamara Park brings you back onto the main route.

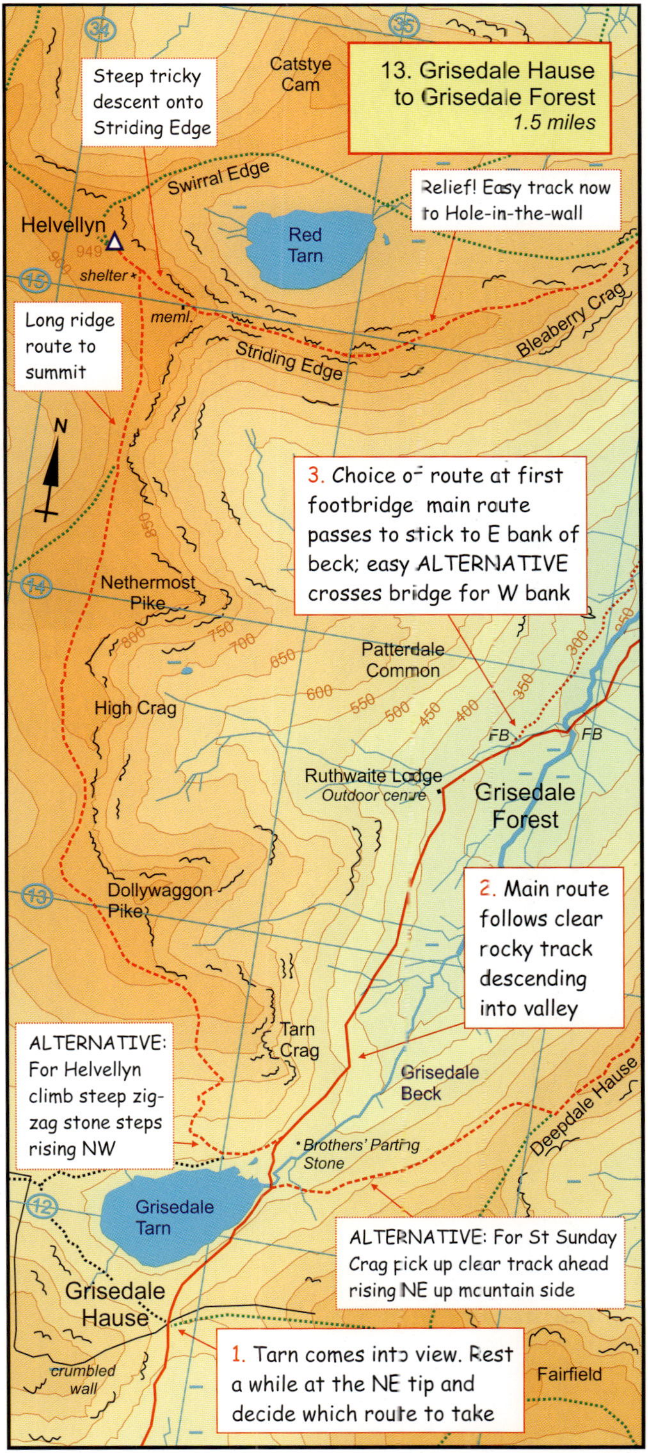

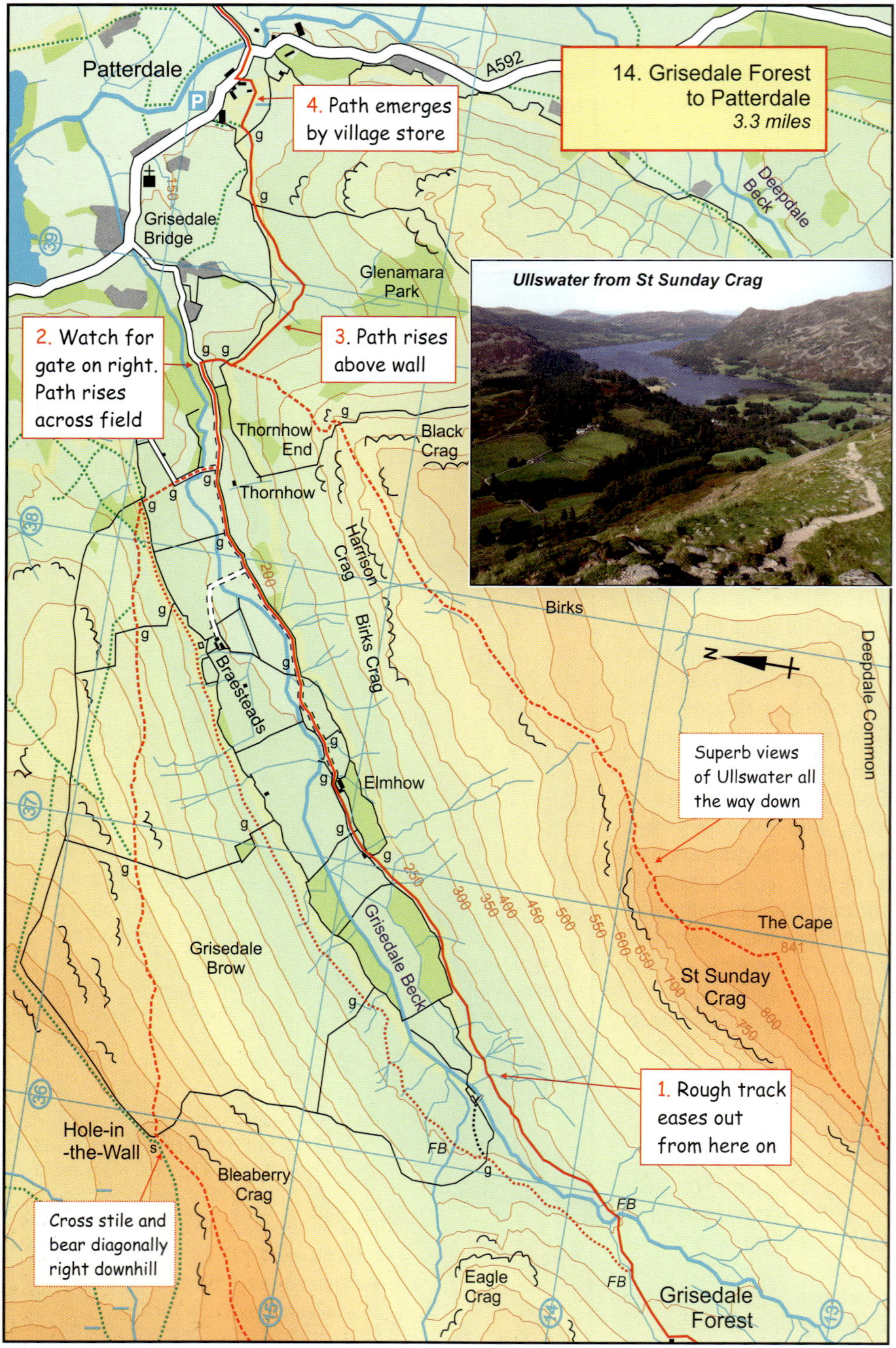

Ullswater from St Sunday Crag

Section 4: **Patterdale to Shap**

15.0 miles (*24.1 km*)

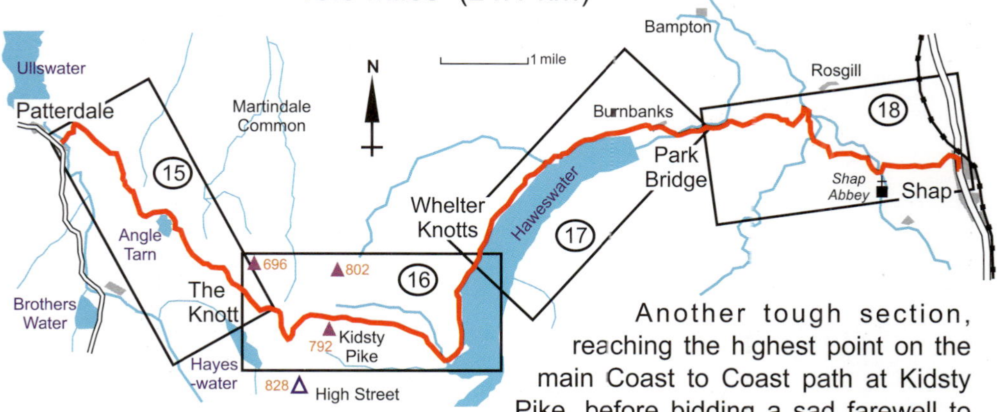

Another tough section, reaching the highest point on the main Coast to Coast path at Kidsty Pike, before bidding a sad farewell to Lakeland. There are no facilities anywhere on today's route, so best stock up before you set off at the village store – a popular gathering point for Coast to Coast walkers.

It's a long steady climb up to Kidsty Pike, but a hearty breakfast should see you at the summit well before noon. The steep descent to Haweswater will take its toll on the legs though, and by the time you reach lake's end you may well have had enough.

Some walkers choose to break the section here by leaving Burnbanks along the road to Bampton, a mile away, otherwise it's onward for the last 4 miles to Shap.

If the weather is really too bad for a high level traverse of High Street, a low level alternative can be made by following the fine lakeside path alongside the southern shore of Ullswater to Howtown, then along the road to Pooley Bridge, where a bridleway heading south east across Moor Divock can be picked up, to join the road leading on to Bampton.

Coast to Coast walkers gather at Patterdale village store

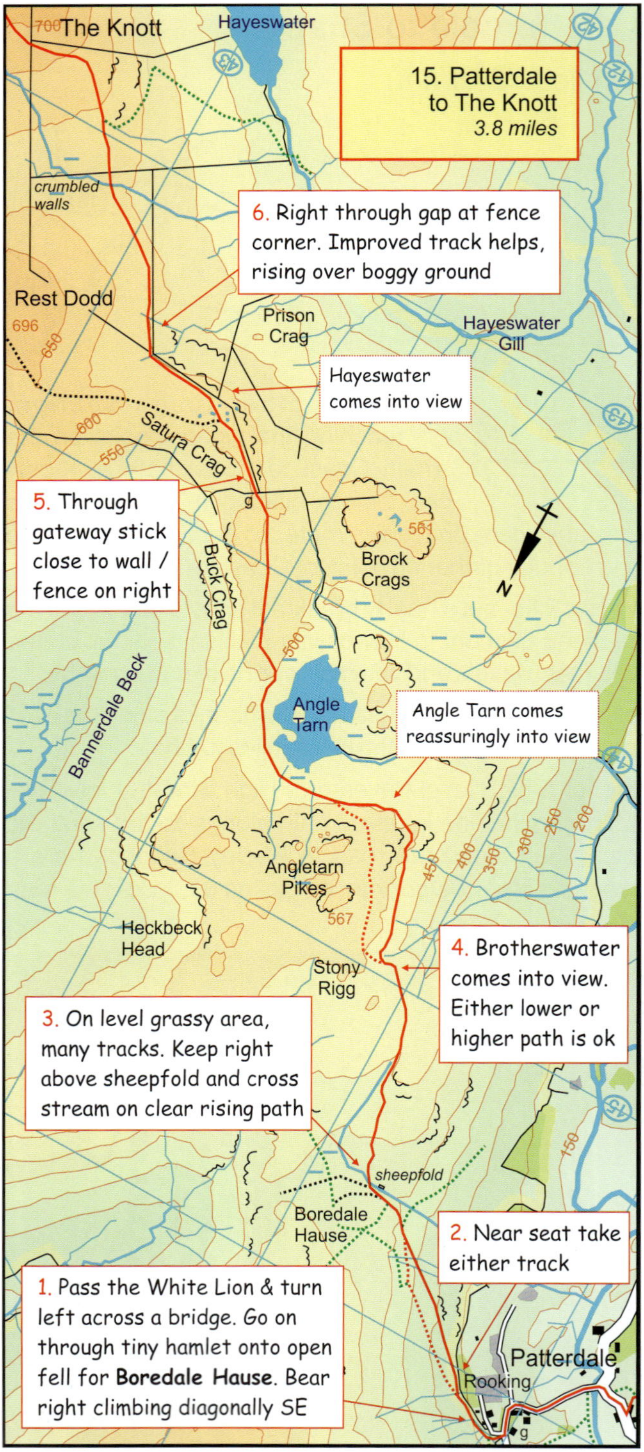

Leave Patterdale, suitably restocked, along the road south for Kirkstone Pass and Windermere. Turn off at a bridge across Goldrill Beck and on through the tiny hamlet of Rooking on to the open fell for **Boredale Hause** and **Angle Tarn**.

There are superb views back across Patterdale, Ullswater and the Hellvellyn range beyond.

Some care is needed as the track levels out at Boredale Hause, where a number of paths split. Take the track bearing right, across the stream above a crumbling sheepfold, heading south, where Brothers Water comes into view. You soon reach the quiet seclusion of Angle Tarn, which is a good place for a short break.

The clear track continues to climb beyond the tarn, with Bannerdale opening below to the left, then Hayeswater appears down to the right. Finally a long steady climb brings you around the shoulder of The Knott and on towards High Street.

Kidsty Pike

With High Street climbing south ahead, watch for a track that cuts off back on the left near a small cairn, taking the Roman Road north over High Raise and on towards Penrith. Turn left and follow this, climbing above Twopenny Crag, curving east for the obvious summit of Kidsty Pike. Linger here a while, enjoying the superb view back of High Street and Riggindale Crags, for this is your last close view of the Lakeland mountains.

The path continues east, dropping sharply down to the craggy outcrop of Kidsty Howes, where a mini scramble takes you steeply downhill towards the shores of Haweswater. Rest a moment by the bridge across the cascading waters of Randale Beck, before continuing north on the long walk along Haweswater's western shore.

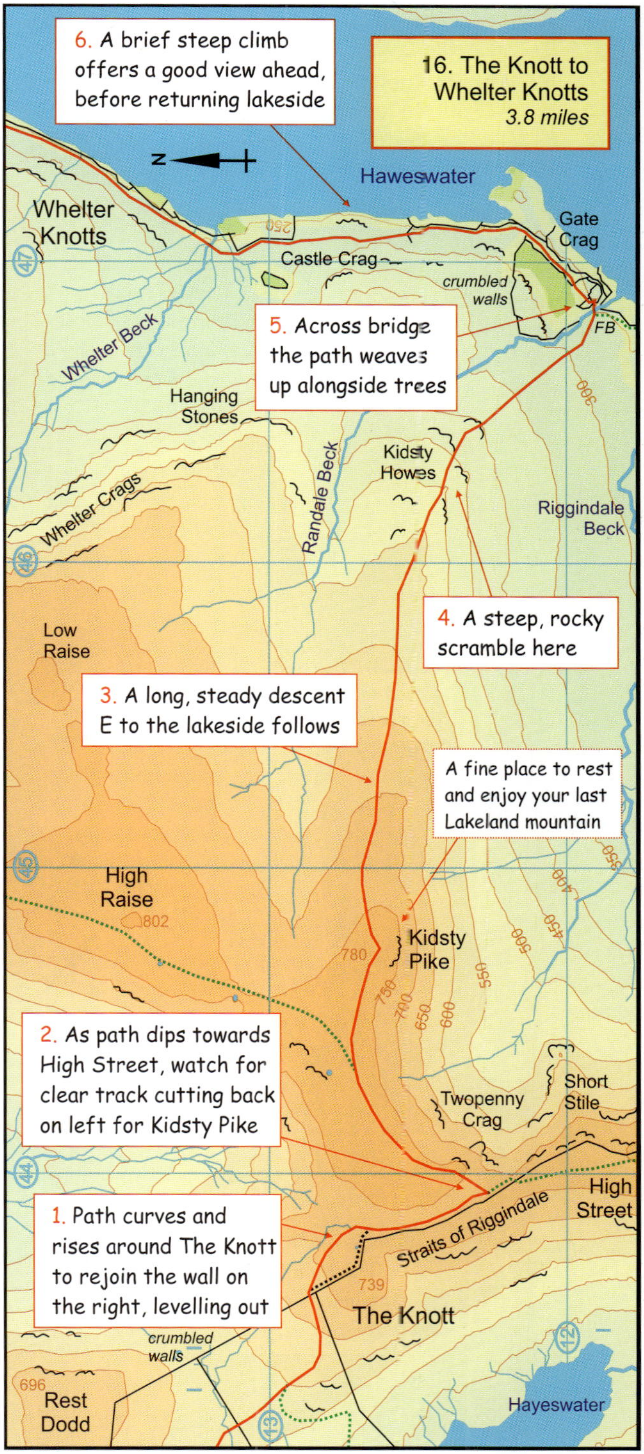

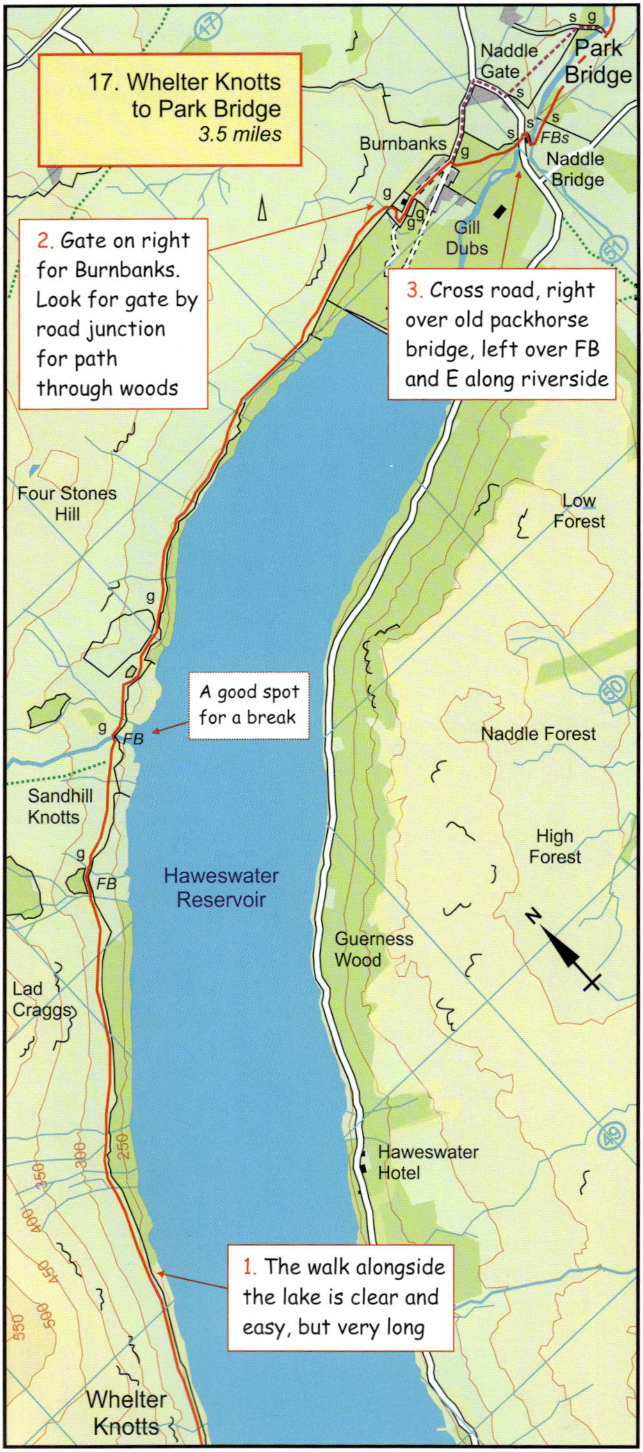

No trouble route finding as the path sticks close to the shoreline. Some temporary high fences and gates have been erected to protect newly planted native woodland from deer.

Haweswater reservoir replaced the original smaller lake in the valley of Mardale in 1940 when Manchester Corporation built a dam at the northern end of the lake, raising the water level by some 30 metres. Measuring 4 miles long (6.5 km) and ½ mile wide, at its maximum capacity the reservoir can hold 84.5 billion litres of water (18.6 billion gallons). The former village of Mardale Green at the head of Haweswater was submerged. During times of drought the remains of the village re-emerge.

You leave the lake beyond the dam and pass through the former dam-builders' village of Burnbanks, built in 1929. At the end of the green by the information board, look for a gate into woods to the south, leading across the road and two footbridges alongside Haweswater Beck to Park Bridge.

The path heads east across fields to join the road by Rosgill Bridge, which it immediately leaves on the right through a gate signed **Coast to Coast**. Follow the wall on the right to a stile by another gate, through which you cut left off the main track to follow a wall, then a fence on the left to a small packhorse bridge. Go up the field and right through some old farm buildings onto the access road. A stile on the left leads you on to **Shap Abbey**.

Little remains of the abbey beyond the western bell tower. From here the access road leads on to the village of Shap.

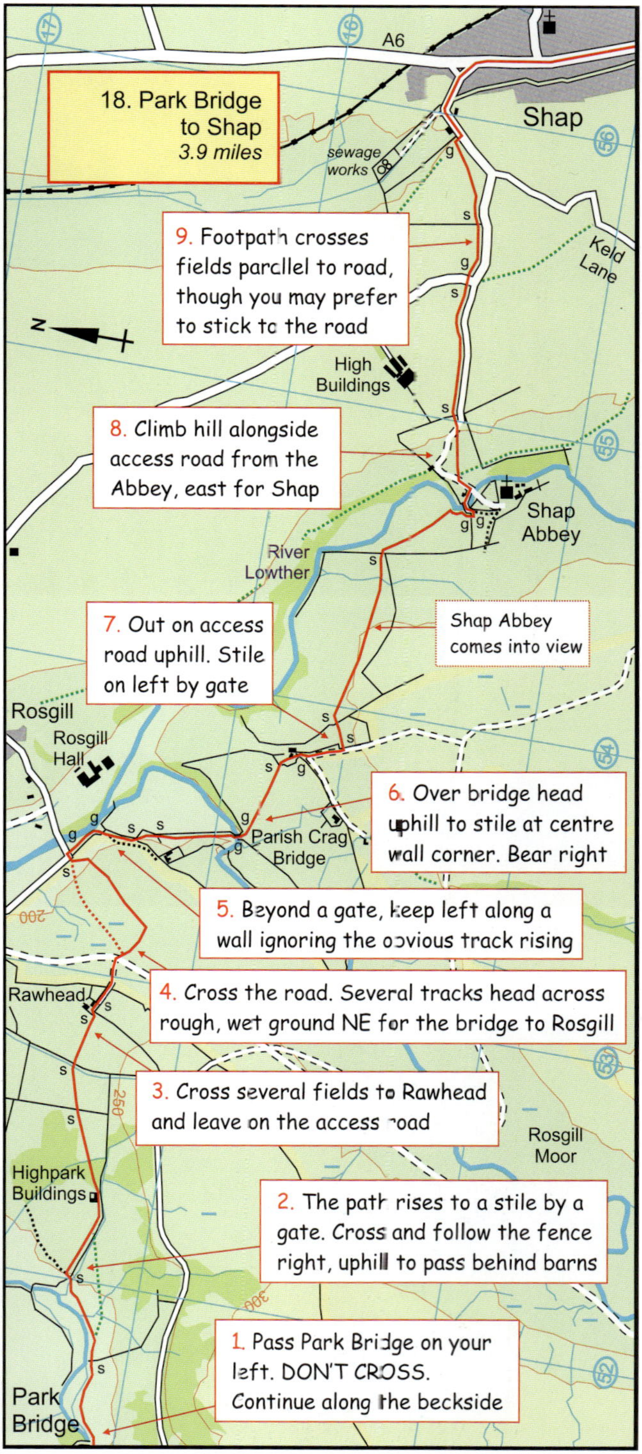

Leaving Patterdale; looking back to Ullswater (top).

The climb past Twopenny Crag for Kidsty Pike (left).

Looking back from Kidsty Pike to Riggindale Head and the Straights of Riggindale (bottom).

Section 5: **Shap to Kirkby Stephen**

19.8 miles (*31.9 km*)

A complete change of landscape now, as the path follows an easy low-level way across a limestone plateau, with wide open spaces almost empty of all habitation.

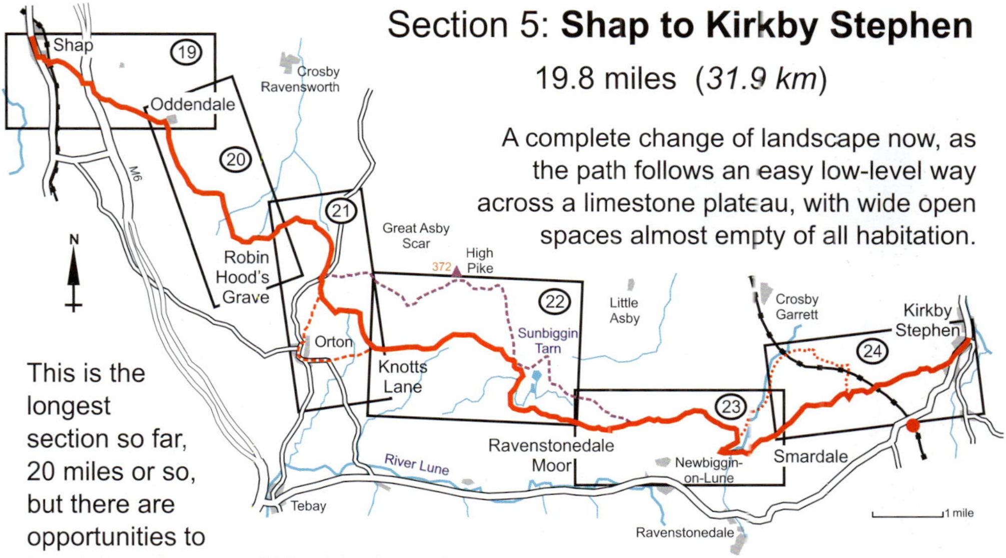

This is the longest section so far, 20 miles or so, but there are opportunities to break it at Orton and Newbiggin-on-Lune.

Wainwright's original route crossed Great Asby Scar, a National Nature Reserve. Now designated Open Access Land it is again accessible (with minor diversions), but is best saved for a return visit, when it can be explored at leisure; it makes a fine circular day's walk from Orton. Today Coast to Coast walkers are advised to stick to the modern route, which is now firmly established, is shorter, quicker and much easier, and offers amenities and accommodation in and around nearby Orton.

Proposed extensions to the Yorkshire Dales National Park may see most of this entire section, between Oddendale and Greenriggs, fall within the new boundaries.

Smardale Gill

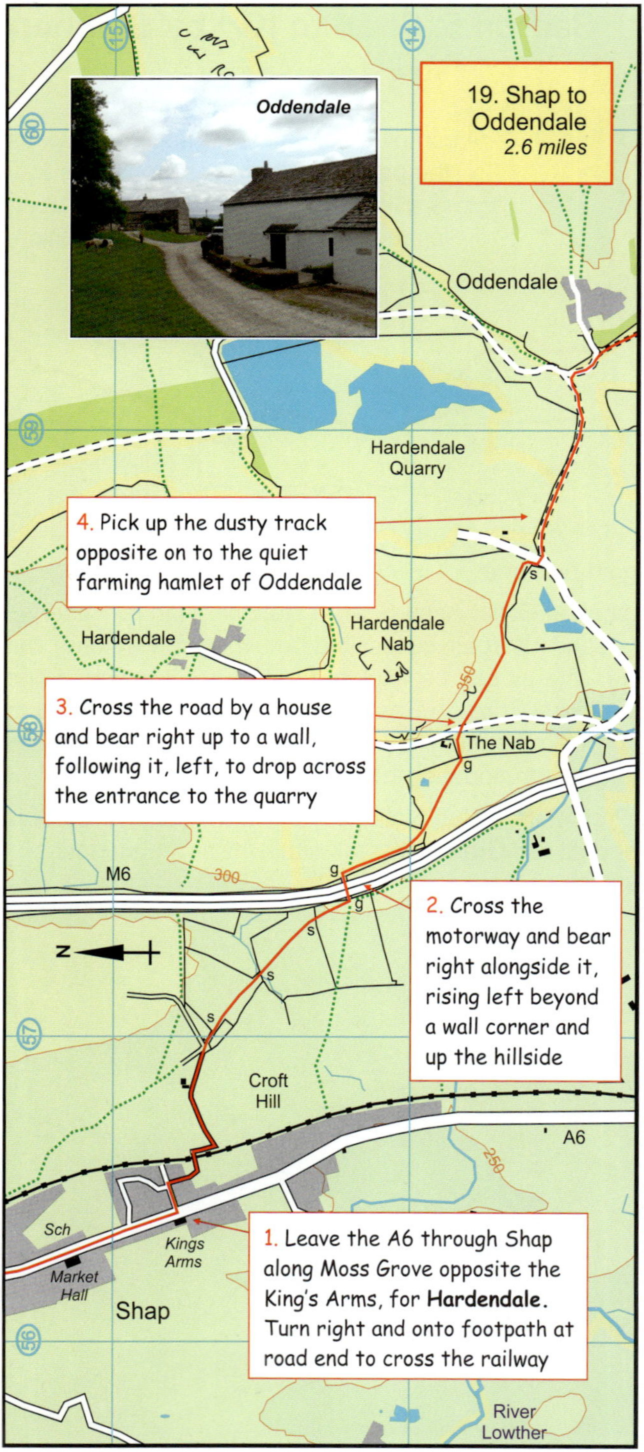

Shap Market Hall

Shap village is more than a mile long, stretched out along the A6. The exit point is half way down, past the school on the left, with the pretty 17th century market hall opposite – built almost entirely from stone purloined from the ruined abbey.

Take a left turn opposite the Kings Arms onto Moss Grove and turn right through a housing estate to cross the railway, and then up to the M6.

The M6 is the longest motorway in England. The stage around Preston was the first motorway built in the country in 1958. The Lancaster to Penrith section was opened in 1970, with the section across Shap Fell being the highest in the country (320 m). Shap's importance as a key travellers' stopping point on the A6 was gone.

The M6 is an important landmark on the Coast to Coast - a third of the route is now done. Continue on past Hardendale Quarry to the secluded hamlet of Oddendale.

Take the clear track south from Oddendale to pass a small plantation, then bear southeast to pass the corner of another. The paths are not always clear here, but are well waymarked. The path rises to cross the line of a Roman road and on to a limestone outcrop at the hill brow. The path now dips past an enormous erratic boulder to cross Lyvennet Beck.

Nearby at the beck's source stands the Black Dub Monument, erected to mark the point where Charles II rested his Scottish army on 8 August 1651, on his way to defeat at the hands of Cromwell in the battle of Worcester on 3 September.

Continue southeast to a wall corner and follow this round eastwards.

The path dips into a shallow dry valley where, a little way along, a cairn marks the spot of Robin Hood's Grave. Could this really be the resting place of England's best loved outlaw?

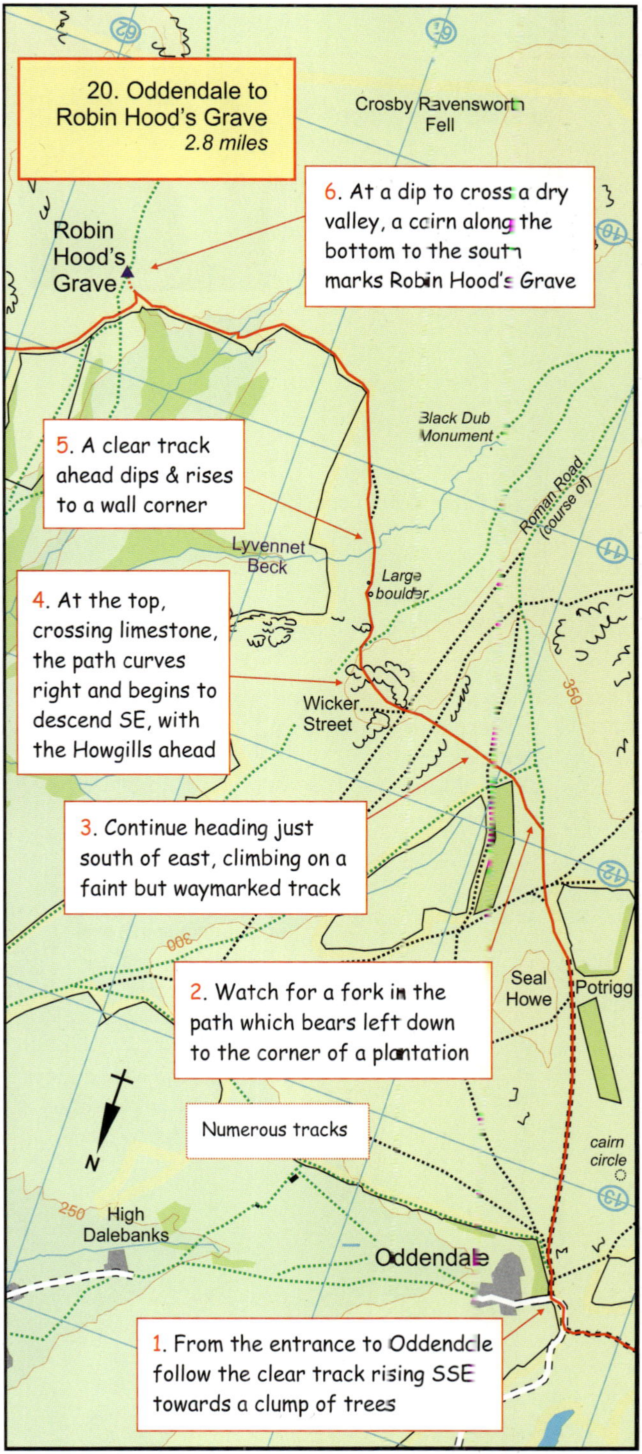

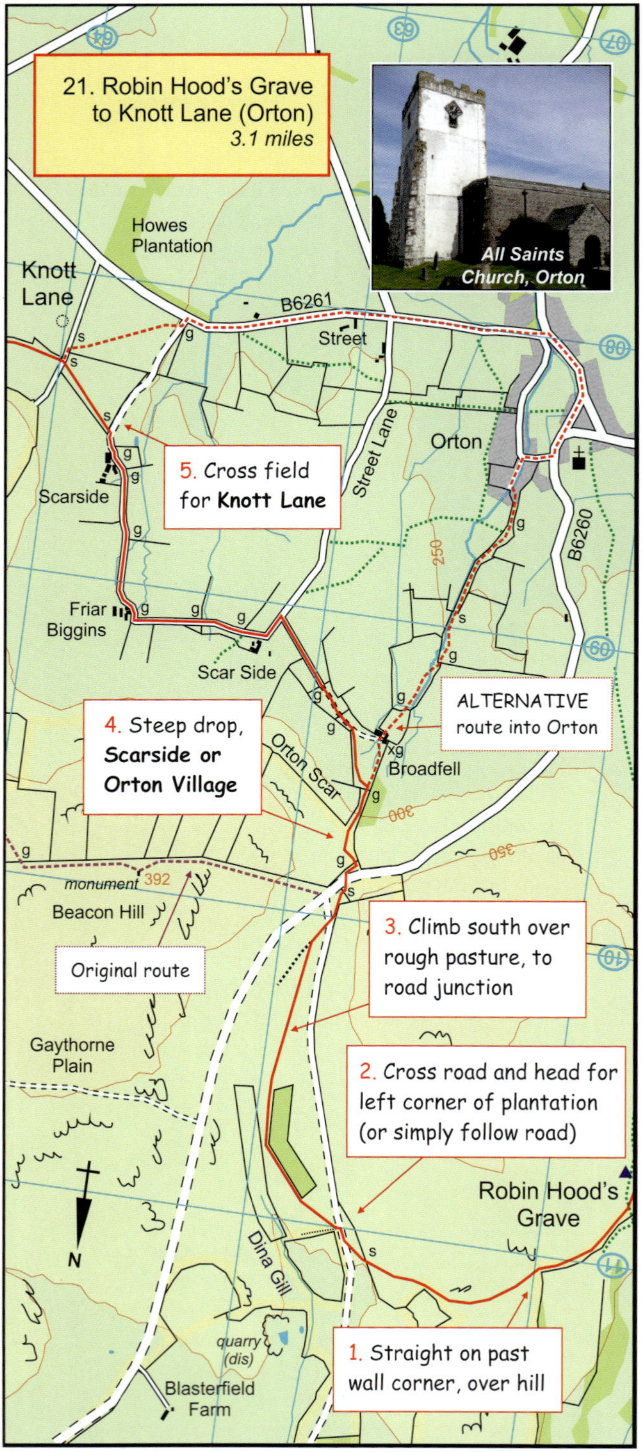

The path bears east over the hill and down to the Crosby Ravensworth road, then turns south to the junction with the road from Appleby.

The original route bore east from here onto Beacon Hill and its monument.

The modern route bears south, then east beneath Orton Scar and onto Knott Lane, with the option of a diversion into the fine Westmorland village of Orton, with all its facilities.

From Knott Lane the path bears east, across fields and stiles to the farm at Acres, and on the road to Sunbiggin, continuing across Tarn Moor to Sunbiggin Tarn. This is a quiet, secluded place. Once the annual nesting spot for 10,000 black headed gulls, they disappeared in 1998, never to return. No-one knows why.

Take the road south to follow the better modern route as it curves east below Tarn Sike and on across Ravenstonedale Moor.

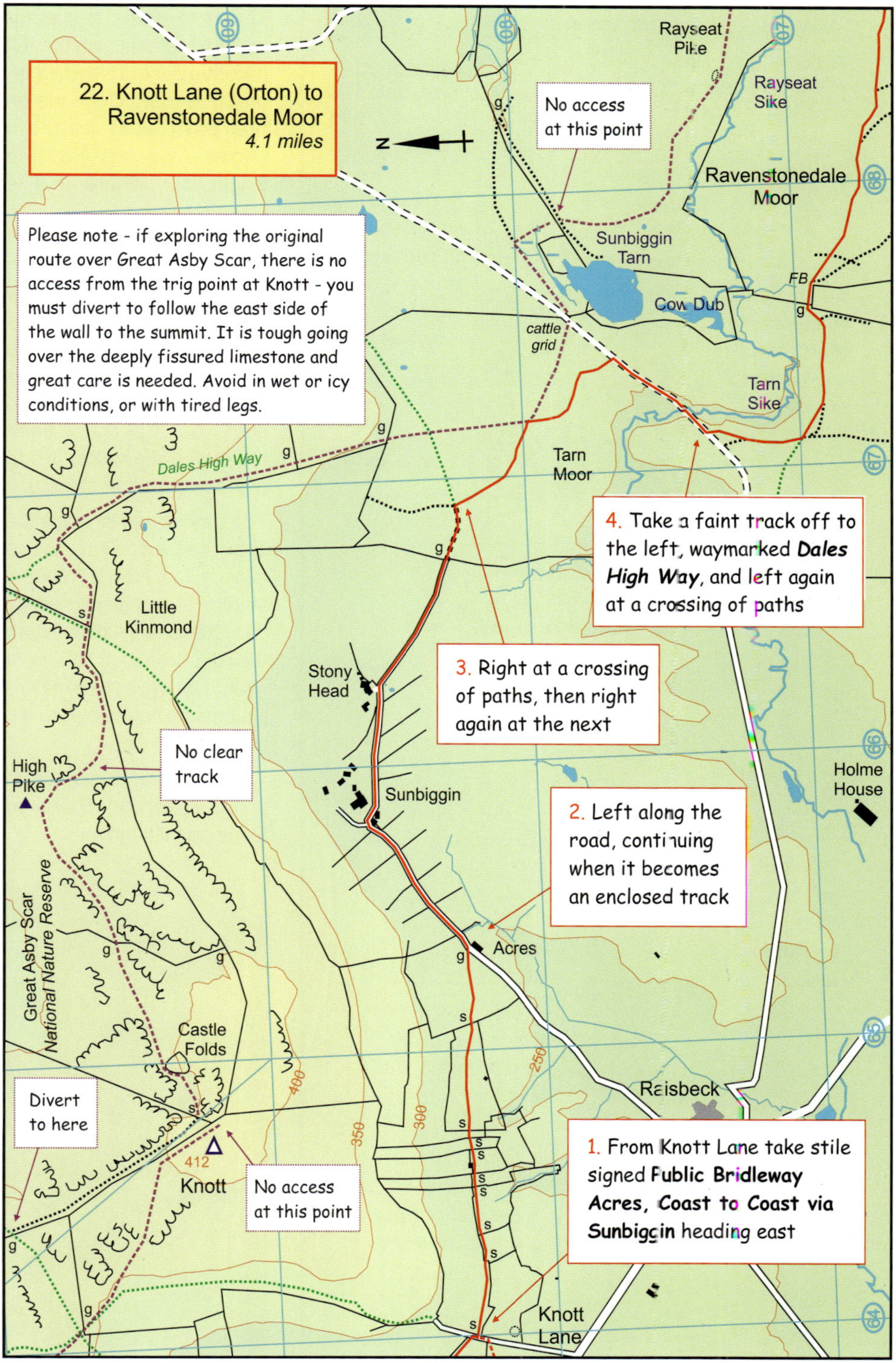
22. Knott Lane (Orton) to Ravenstonedale Moor
4.1 miles
Please note - if exploring the original route over Great Asby Scar, there is no access from the trig point at Knott - you must divert to follow the east side of the wall to the summit. It is tough going over the deeply fissured limestone and great care is needed. Avoid in wet or icy conditions, or with tired legs.
1. From Knott Lane take stile signed Public Bridleway Acres, Coast to Coast via Sunbiggin heading east
2. Left along the road, continuing when it becomes an enclosed track
3. Right at a crossing of paths, then right again at the next
4. Take a faint track off to the left, waymarked Dales High Way, and left again at a crossing of paths
No access at this point
No access at this point
No clear track
Divert to here
Rayseat Pike
Rayseat Sike
Ravenstonedale Moor
Sunbiggin Tarn
Cow Dub
FB
cattle grid
Tarn Sike
Tarn Moor
Dales High Way
Little Kinmond
Stony Head
Sunbiggin
High Pike
Holme House
Acres
Great Asby Scar National Nature Reserve
Castle Folds
Raisbeck
Knott
412
Knott Lane
400
350
300
250
69
70
68
67
66
65
64

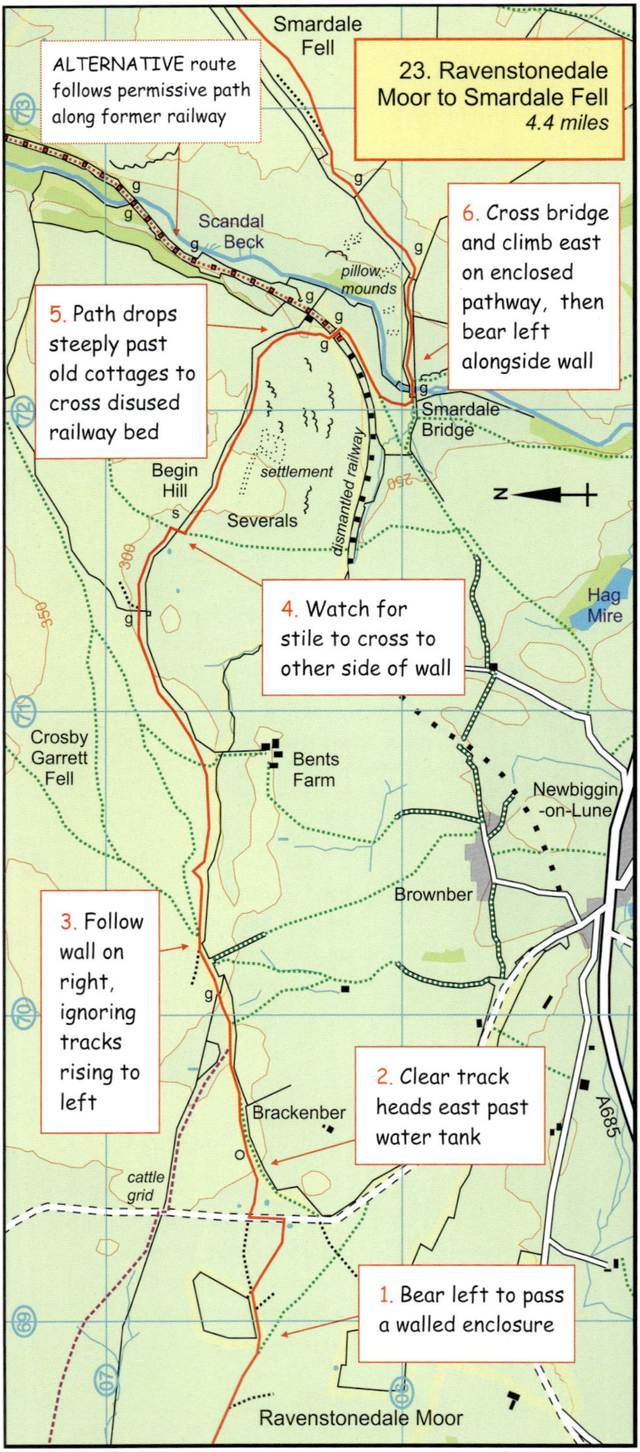

The path drops to pass a walled enclosure on the left and on up to the Newbiggin-on-Lune road. Continue on the path east beneath Crosby Garrett Fell, to Begin Hill, where a stile leads you across the wall. This is an area of important Romano-British settlements, known as the Severals. The original route crossed straight across the archaeological remains (not that there's much to see), but has now been redirected along the inside of the wall to protect them.

The path drops to cross the dismantled Stainmore railway line. Now a National Nature Reserve owned by the Cumbria Wildlife Trust, the old trackbed offers a fine level alternative permissive route to Smardale.

The path now descends to cross Scandal Beck at Smardale Bridge.

The path follows the wall on the left up onto Smardale Fell, continuing to climb east over the hill brow where the wall drops away to the left, clearly signed **Coast to Coast**. On a clear day there are excellent long views of the Eden Valley ahead, and the Pennine mountain range, including Mallerstang and Wild Boar Fell off to the right.

Upon reaching the road turn right, then left at the junction, watching for a stile on the right. The path heads east to round a wall corner on to a railway underpass. The signs of more ancient village settlements can clearly be seen beyond the underpass. Continue northeast, across stiles, finally to pass under the former Stainmore railway line at Greenriggs Farm.

Follow the permissive path to the left, around the farm buildings, and out along the access road which leads down behind Kirkby Stephen. Cut right at any point, to join the main road through this popular Pennine market town.

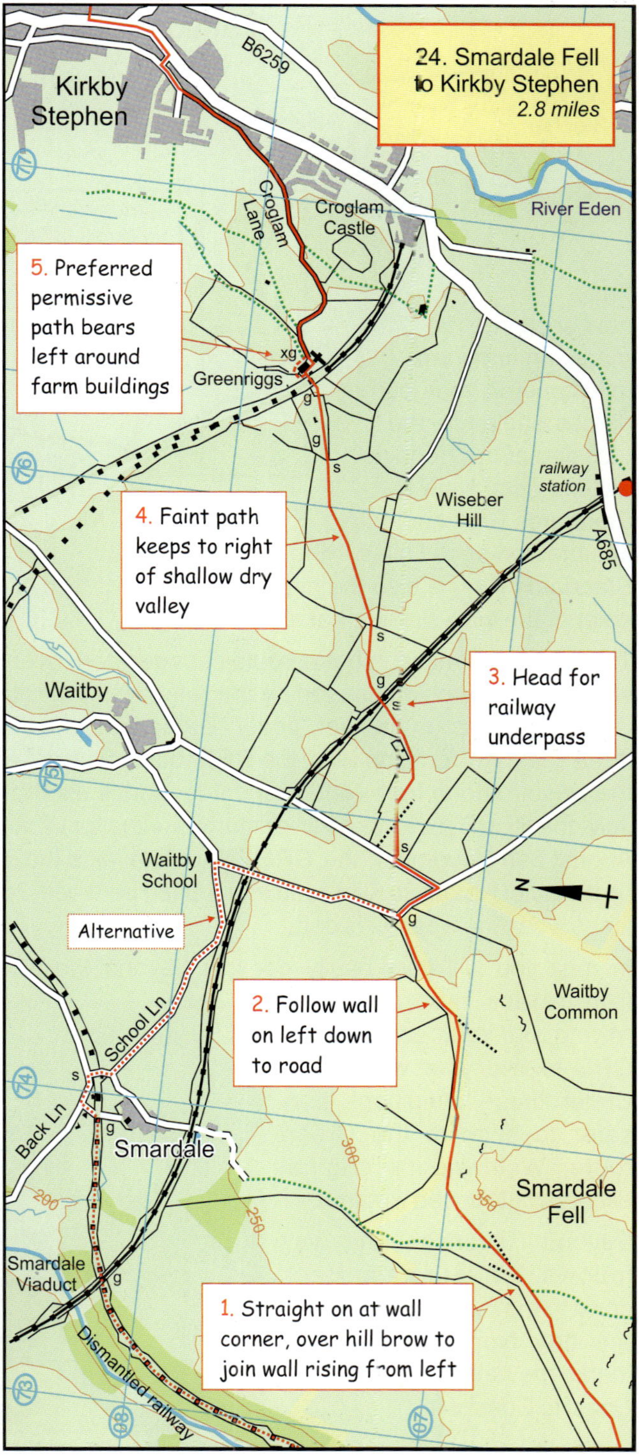

Section 6: **Kirkby Stephen to Keld**

11.3 miles (*18.7 km*)

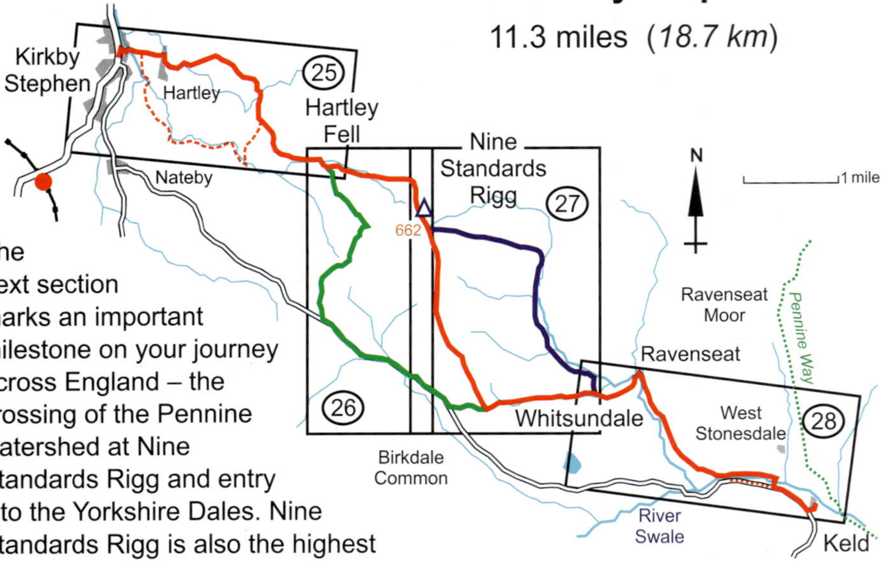

The next section marks an important milestone on your journey across England – the crossing of the Pennine watershed at Nine Standards Rigg and entry into the Yorkshire Dales. Nine Standards Rigg is also the highest point of the walk outside Lakeland.

There have been a number of route changes here over the years, to avoid the worst effects of the erosion caused by the relentless passage of thousands of Coast-to-Coasters' boots on the wet, peaty heather moorland. Today the walk divides into three seasonal route options: the **RED** route follows Wainwright's original way along the western ridge from Nine Standards, and is used by walkers between May and July; the **BLUE** route takes an easterly beeline for Whitsundale and is used between August and November; the **GREEN** route avoids the summit altogether by picking up the quiet Nateby to Keld road and is used between December and April, or at other times when the weather is bad.

In mist you will very easily get lost beyond the Nine Standards on the broad featureless moorland top, relying on your compass or GPS to find your way down. Under these conditions it is safer to stick to the Green route, Wainwright's original escape route in bad weather.

Nine Standards

Beyond Ravenseat the way follows Whitsundale Beck down to the Keld road and on to the tiny Norse village that marks the halfway point on the Coast to Coast walk.

Frank's Bridge

Leave Kirkby Stephen marketplace by the church cloisters, heading east along Stoneshot, to cross the River Eden at Frank's Bridge. Follow the wall on your left to Hartley. Here turn right along the road up to the quarry entrance, bearing left to follow the road as it climbs steadily above the quarry and out onto the open fell.

The path curves to join another wall and on up to a signpost which marks the first seasonal split point: continue along the bridleway for the GREEN route, or turn left to climb alongside Faraday Gill for the RED & BLUE routes.

Standards in mist

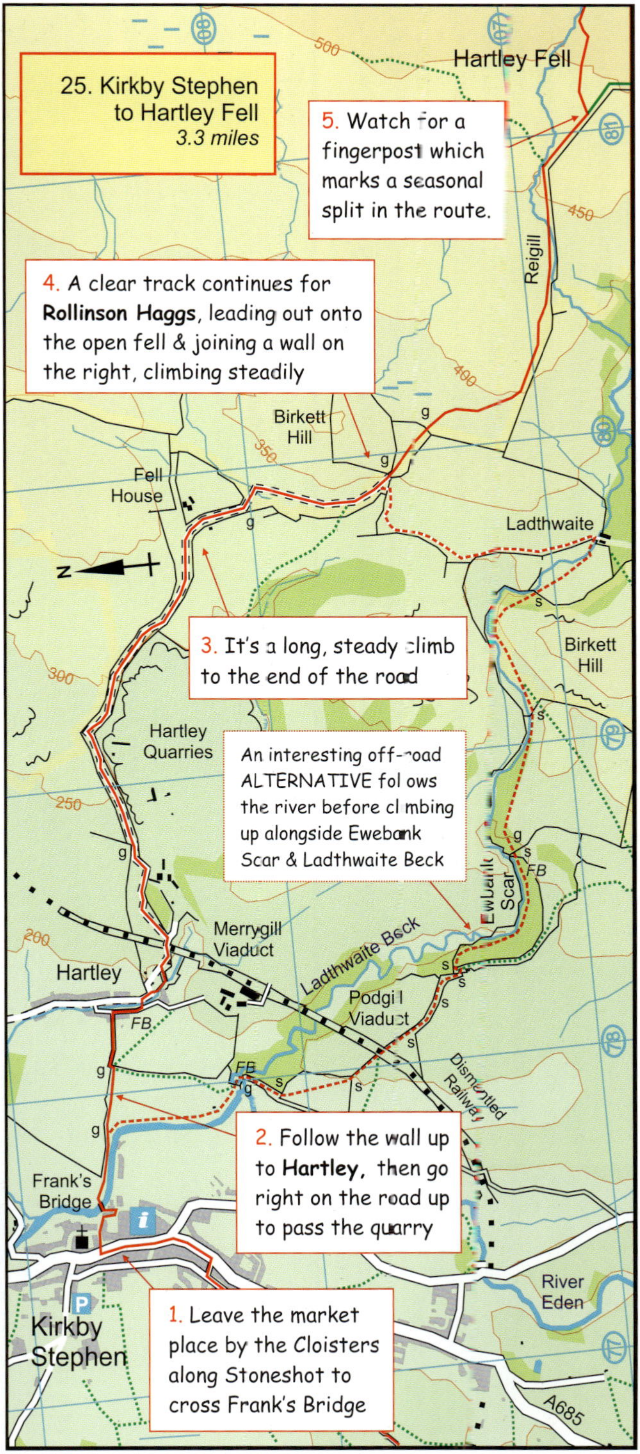

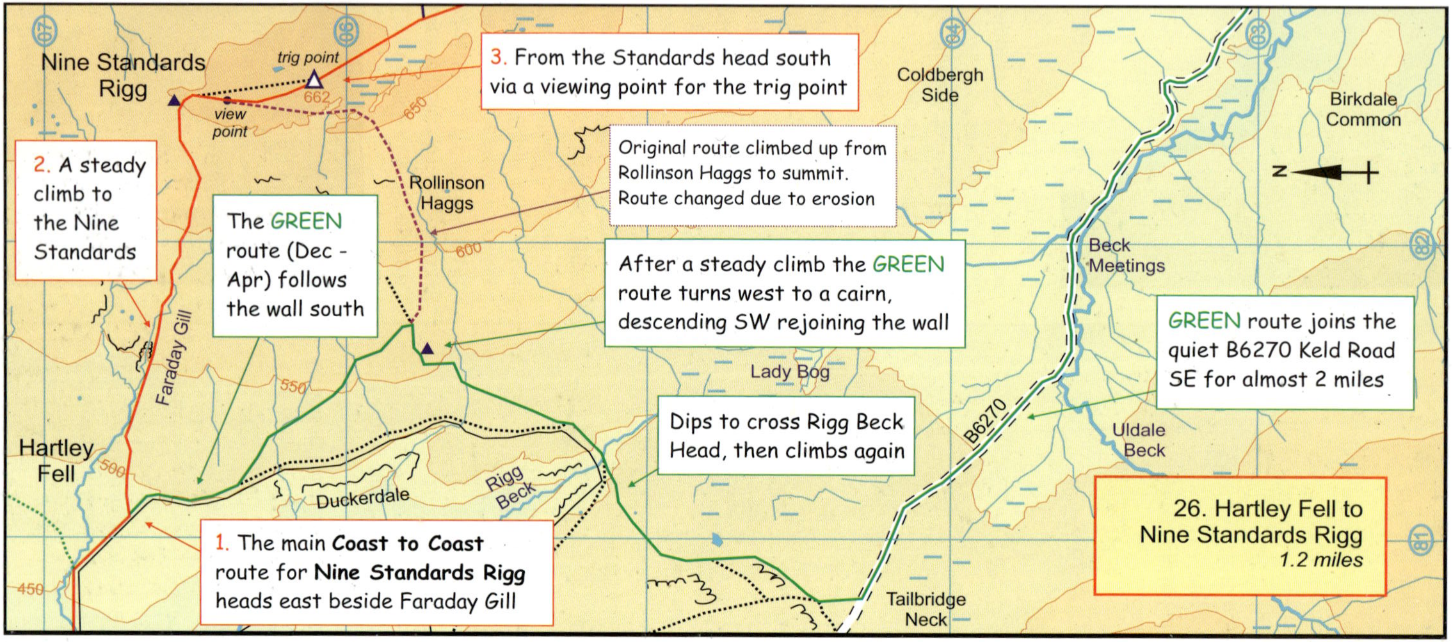

The trek up to the Nine Standards is short and straightforward. No-one is sure why these cairns were built, but one theory has it they were meant to look like an army encampment from the valley below, to deter Scots invaders. A short stroll south brings you to the trig point and the summit of Nine Standards Rigg.

There are superb views from here (a nearby viewpoint helps identify the sights). The path then continues to the boggy quagmire at the head of Backstone Beck. The RED and BLUE routes separate beyond this, so there's no avoiding it. The RED route continues south along the ridge, descending beyond the pillar at Millstones to join a shooting track heading east, where the GREEN route rejoins. The BLUE route heads just south of east (bearing about 100 degrees), descending slowly across boggy tracts before turning south alongside Whitsundale Beck. All paths rejoin at Ney Gill.

Millstones

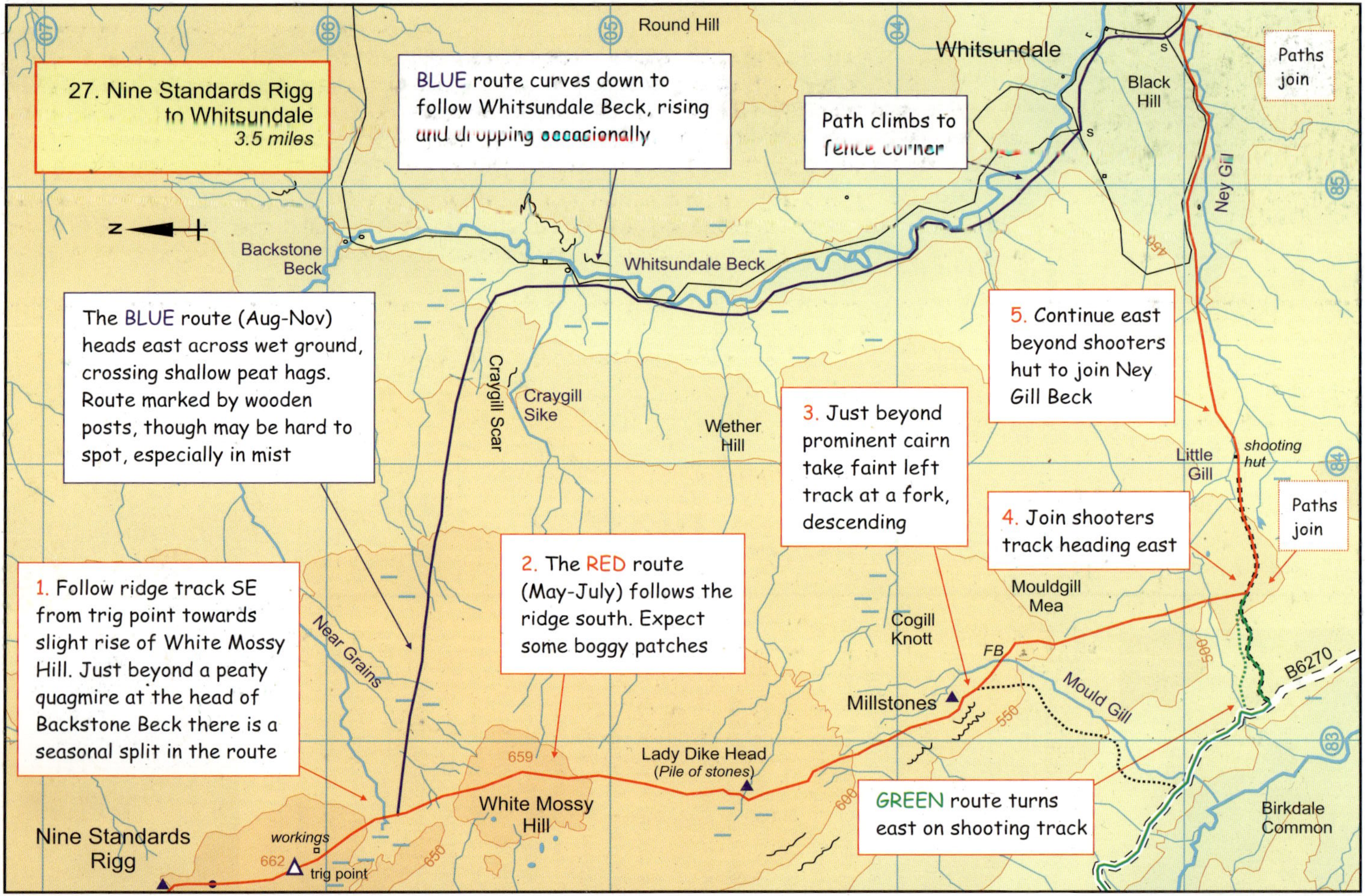

27. Nine Standards Rigg to Whitsundale
3.5 miles
N
The BLUE route (Aug-Nov) heads east across wet ground, crossing shallow peat hags. Route marked by wooden posts, though may be hard to spot, especially in mist
BLUE route curves down to follow Whitsundale Beck, rising and dropping occasionally
Path climbs to fence corner
Paths join
1. Follow ridge track SE from trig point towards slight rise of White Mossy Hill. Just beyond a peaty quagmire at the head of Backstone Beck there is a seasonal split in the route
2. The RED route (May-July) follows the ridge south. Expect some boggy patches
3. Just beyond prominent cairn take faint left track at a fork, descending
4. Join shooters track heading east
5. Continue east beyond shooters hut to join Ney Gill Beck
GREEN route turns east on shooting track
Paths join
Round Hill
Whitsundale
Black Hill
Backstone Beck
Whitsundale Beck
Ney Gill
Craygill Scar
Craygill Sike
Wether Hill
Little Gill
shooting hut
Near Grains
Mouldgill Mea
Cogill Knott
FB
Millstones
Mould Gill
B6270
Lady Dike Head
(Pile of stones)
White Mossy Hill
Nine Standards Rigg
workings
trig point
662
650
659
600
550
500
450
Birkdale Common
07
06
05
04
85
84
83

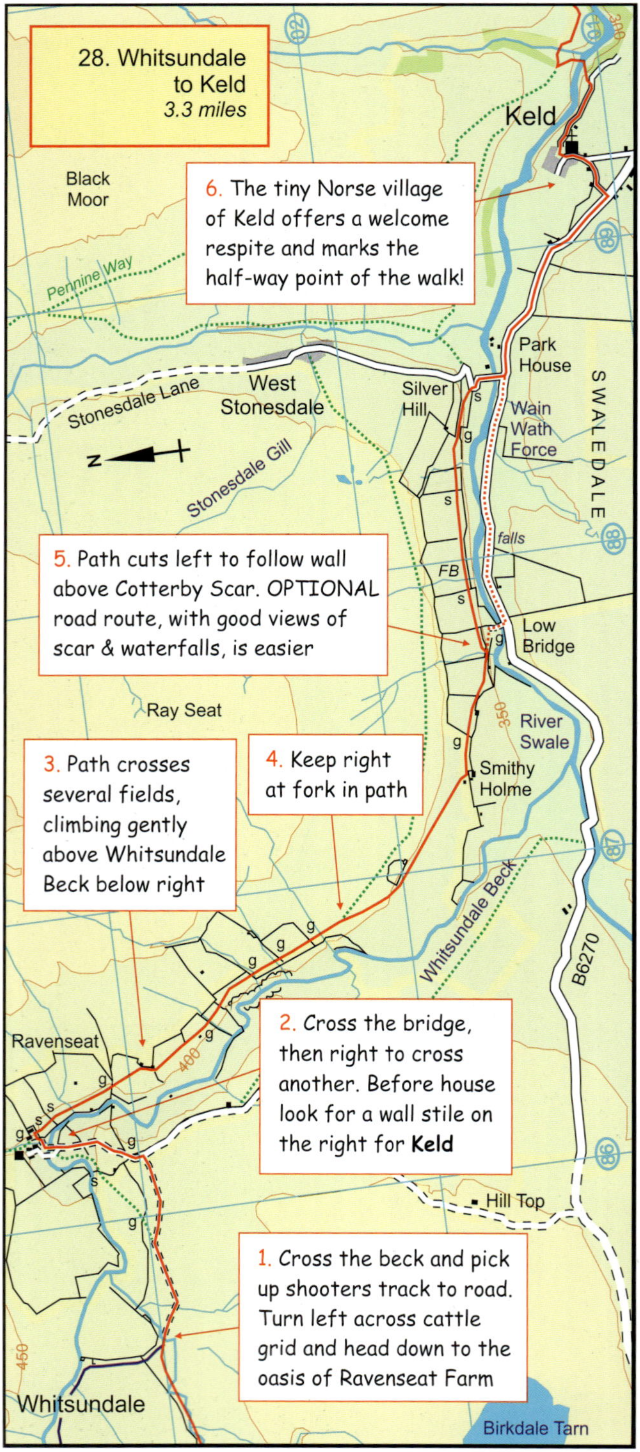

The tiny farming hamlet of Ravenseat is a welcome sight, and with luck you may even find refreshments at the farm.

The path crosses two bridges here and then picks up a track heading southeast across fields above Whitsundale Beck, which surges over a waterfall and cuts deeply and impressively into the valley below at a ravine at How Edge.

The path drops towards the road beyond a farmhouse at Smithy Holme, but cuts back left to cross fields above Cotterby Scar. However, you may prefer to join the road to Keld here, for the fine views of the limestone scar and waterfalls.

The road continues uphill to Keld, where a left turn takes you down into the village centre.

"Always, at Keld, there is the music of the river" - AW

Keld (above).

East Gill Force, upper falls (left).

East Gill Force, lower falls (below).

Kisdon Force - off route (right).

Falls at Ravenseat (opposite, top)

Wain Wath Force, on the road to Keld (opposite bottom).

Section 7: **Keld to Reeth**

10.7 miles (*17.2 km*)

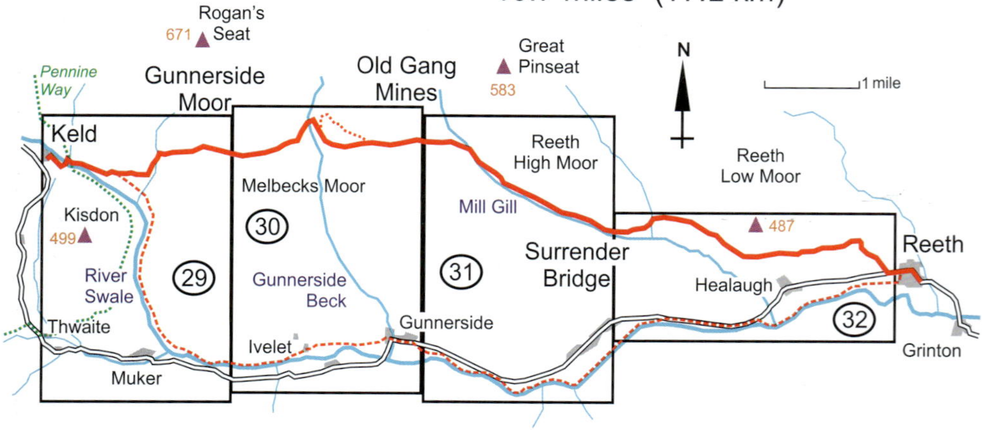

Swaledale, at the northern tip of the Yorkshire Dales, was Wainwright's favourite.

Wainwright offers two routes from Keld to Reeth: the *royal road* follows a gentle, low-level riverside way, adding about a mile. In bad weather this is the way to go.

His preferred route, however, is a fascinating and exciting high-level traverse of the moors - a landscape devastated by lead mining, yet strikingly beautiful. The moors around Gunnerside Gill in particular bear the scars of hushing - a technique widely used in the area in the 18th and 19th centuries to expose lead veins. Water was accumulated behind a high-level turf dam, then released in a flood to scour away surface soil and rocks. Mines, spoil heaps, flues and mill ruins abound.

Leave Keld on a narrow track signed for **Kisdon Force** and **Muker**, soon forking left on the **Pennine Way** to cross the river. The lower East Gill falls can be seen by taking a gate on the right by the footbridge, the higher falls are passed on the way up to another bridge where the Coast to Coast and Pennine Way part company.

The path then climbs up to the ruins of Crackpot Hall, where a decision of routes must be made. Bear left on a track that climbs above the ruin for Swinner Gill and the high-level route, or continue straight on for a gentle low-level riverside route.

Blakethwaite Smelt Mill

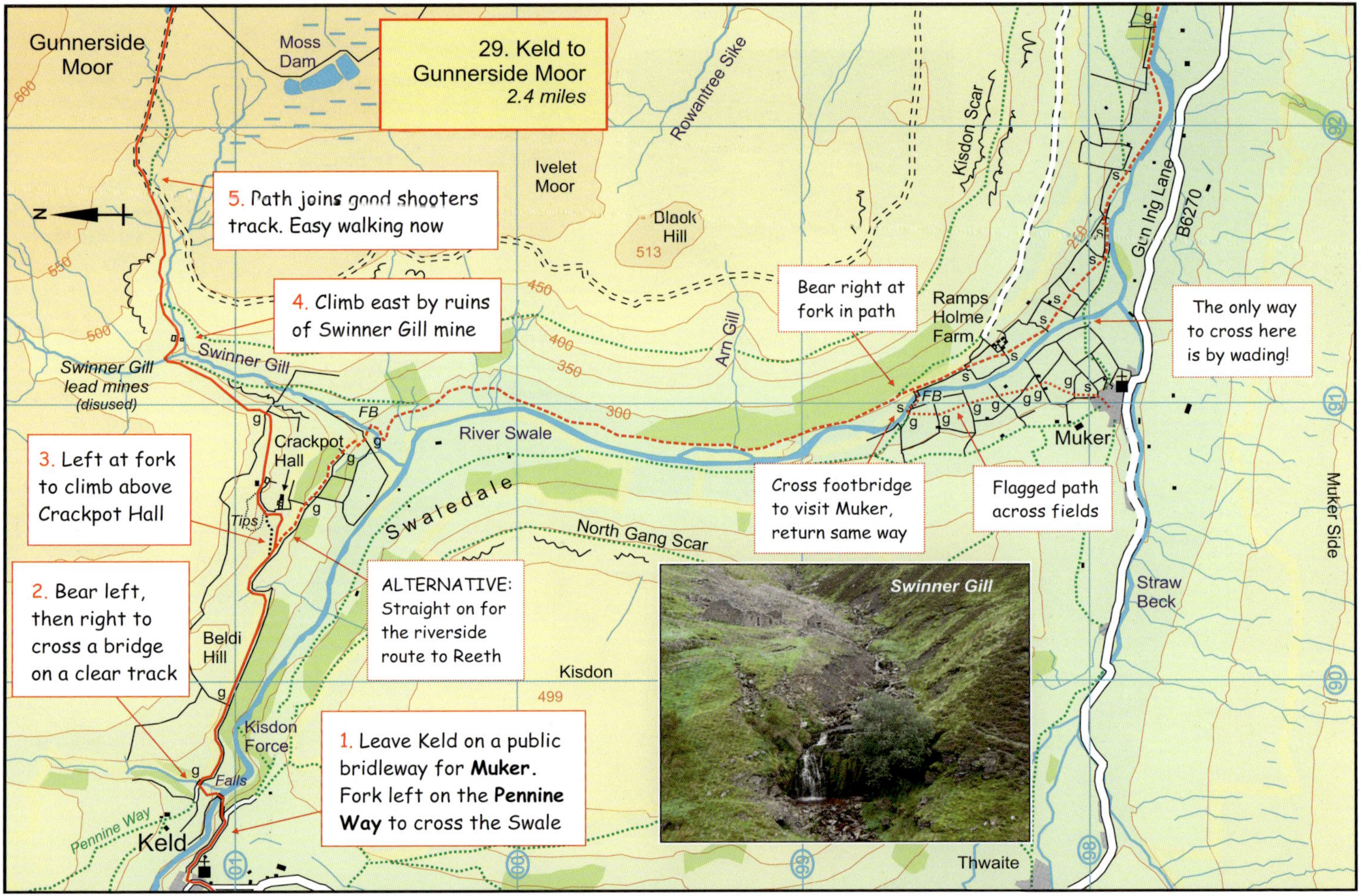
29. Keld to Gunnerside Moor
2.4 miles
1. Leave Keld on a public bridleway for **Muker**. Fork left on the **Pennine Way** to cross the Swale
2. Bear left, then right to cross a bridge on a clear track
3. Left at fork to climb above Crackpot Hall
4. Climb east by ruins of Swinner Gill mine
5. Path joins good shooters track. Easy walking now
ALTERNATIVE: Straight on for the riverside route to Reeth
Bear right at fork in path
Cross footbridge to visit Muker, return same way
Flagged path across fields
The only way to cross here is by wading!
Swinner Gill
Gunnerside Moor
Moss Dam
Ivelet Moor
Black Hill
513
Rowantree Sike
Kisdon Scar
Arn Gill
Ramps Holme Farm
Gun Ing Lane
B6270
Muker
Muker Side
Straw Beck
Thwaite
Kisdon
499
North Gang Scar
Swaledale
River Swale
Crackpot Hall
Tips
Swinner Gill
Swinner Gill lead mines (disused)
Beldi Hill
Kisdon Force
Falls
Pennine Way
Keld
FB
N
600
550
500
450
400
350
300
250
91
92
90
99
00
01
98

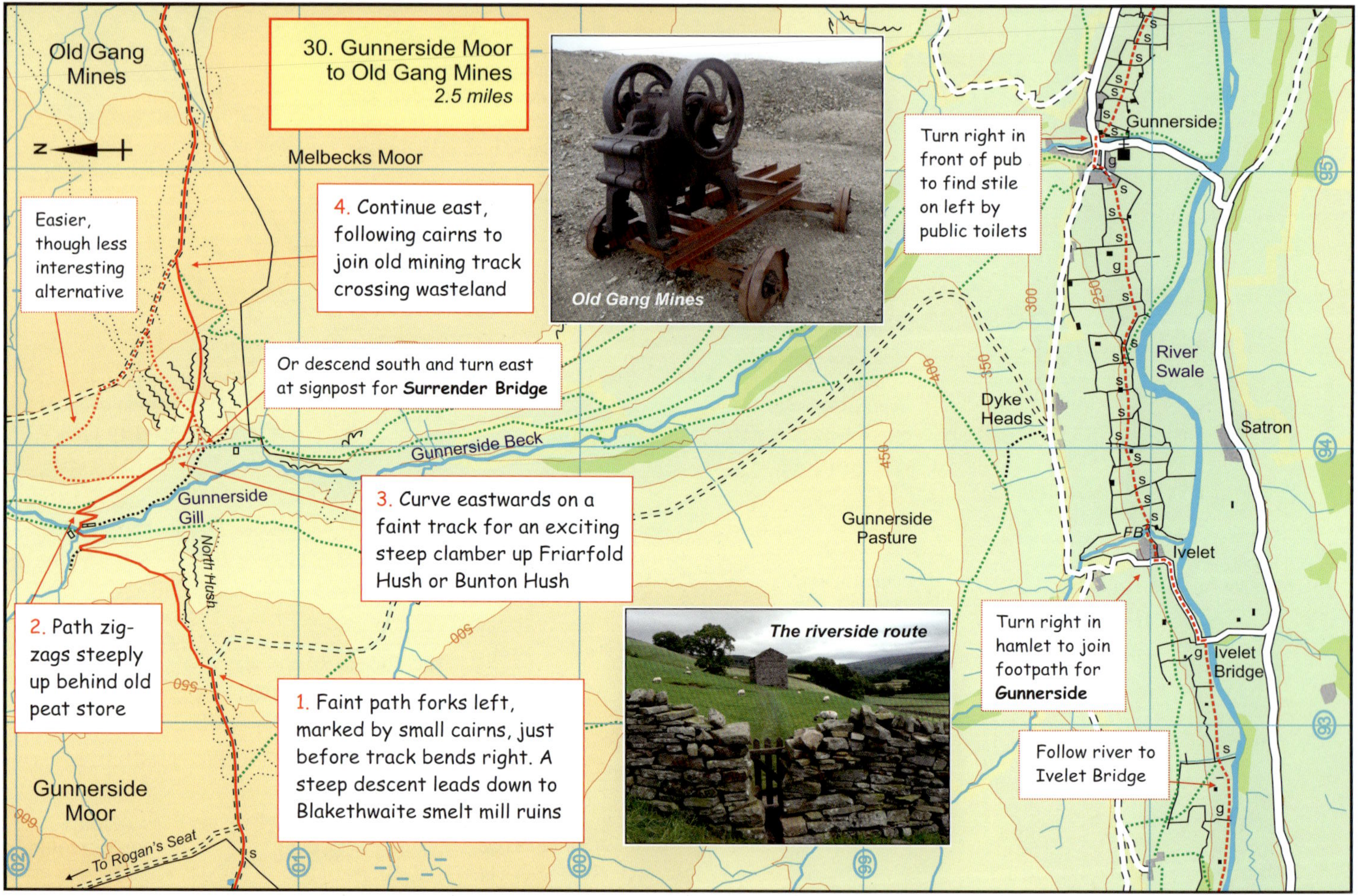
30. Gunnerside Moor to Old Gang Mines
2.5 miles
Old Gang Mines
N
Melbecks Moor
Easier, though less interesting alternative
4. Continue east, following cairns to join old mining track crossing wasteland
Or descend south and turn east at signpost for **Surrender Bridge**
3. Curve eastwards on a faint track for an exciting steep clamber up Friarfold Hush or Bunton Hush
2. Path zig-zags steeply up behind old peat store
1. Faint path forks left, marked by small cairns, just before track bends right. A steep descent leads down to Blakethwaite smelt mill ruins
Gunnerside Beck
Gunnerside Gill
North Hush
Gunnerside Moor
To Rogan's Seat
Old Gang Mines
The riverside route
Gunnerside Pasture
Dyke Heads
Turn right in front of pub to find stile on left by public toilets
Gunnerside
River Swale
Satron
Ivelet
FB
Turn right in hamlet to join footpath for **Gunnerside**
Ivelet Bridge
Follow river to Ivelet Bridge
02
01
00
99
93
94
95
600
550
500
450
400
350
300
250

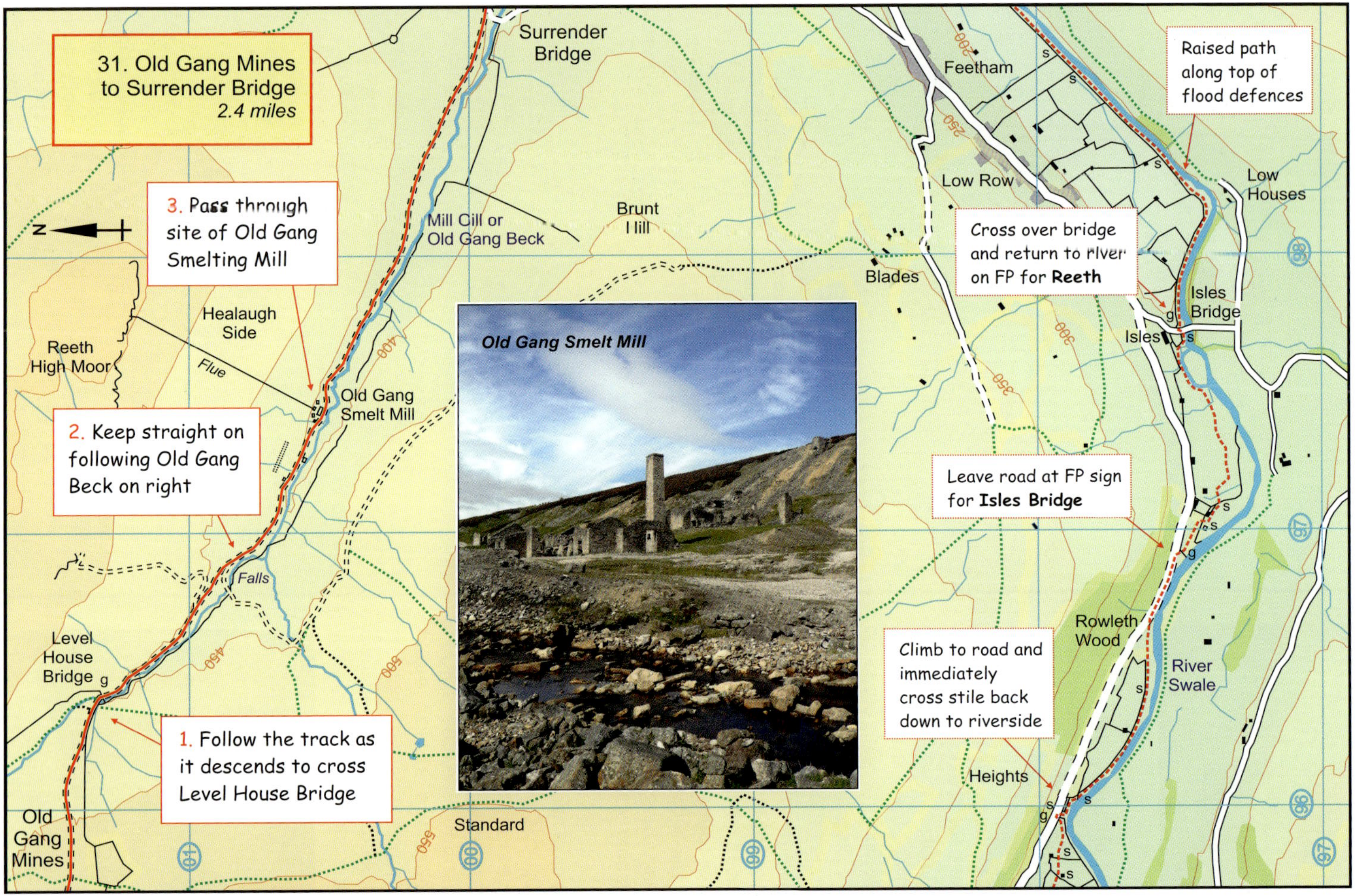
31. Old Gang Mines to Surrender Bridge
2.4 miles
N
1. Follow the track as it descends to cross Level House Bridge
2. Keep straight on following Old Gang Beck on right
3. Pass through site of Old Gang Smelting Mill
Cross over bridge and return to river on FP for Reeth
Leave road at FP sign for Isles Bridge
Climb to road and immediately cross stile back down to riverside
Raised path along top of flood defences
Old Gang Smelt Mill
Surrender Bridge
Mill Gill or Old Gang Beck
Brunt Hill
Healaugh Side
Reeth High Moor
Flue
Old Gang Smelt Mill
Falls
Level House Bridge
Old Gang Mines
Standard
Feetham
Low Row
Blades
Low Houses
Isles Bridge
Isles
Rowleth Wood
River Swale
Heights

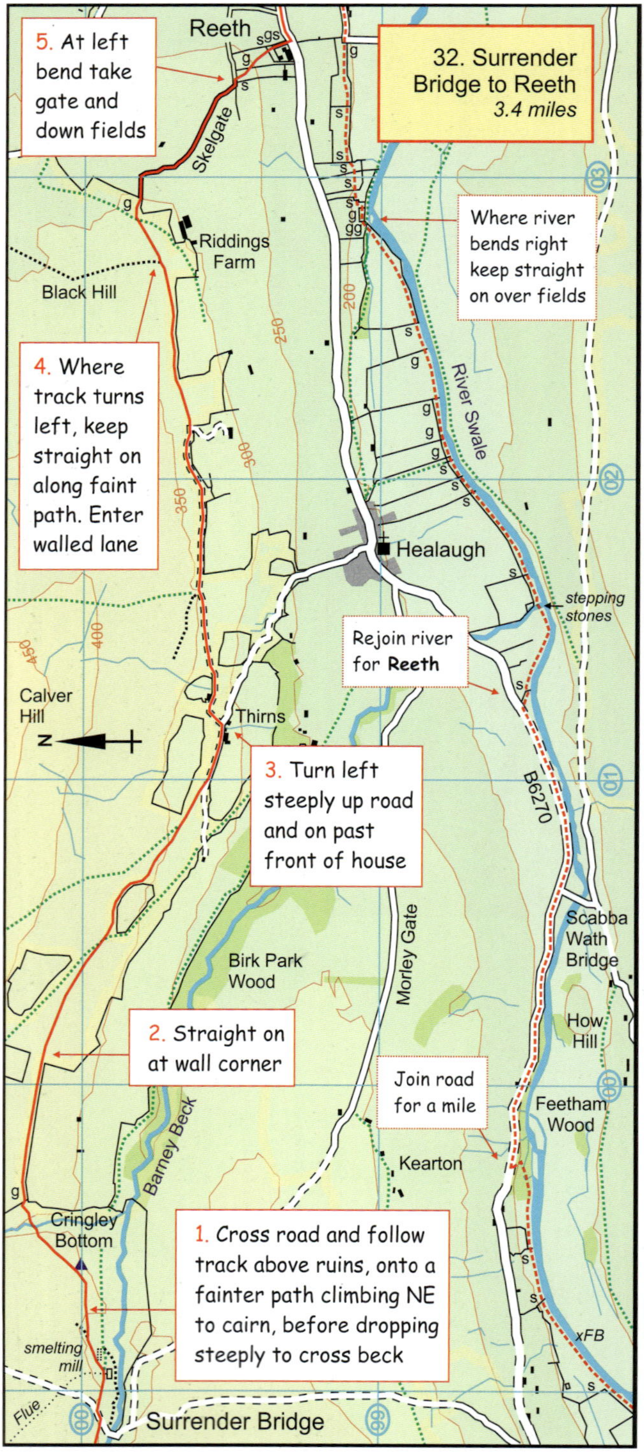

Most of these moors are managed as grouse moors, so don't be surprised to come across shooting parties between August and December. These are usually well organised affairs, and if you stick to the path they will cause you no problems.

The old mine track meets the road above Surrender Bridge. Cross straight over, onto a footpath, bearing left at a fork on a faint track which passes above the old ruined Smelt Mill, over wet ground, and up to a cairn. Beyond is a steep drop to cross the beck at Cringley Bottom. The path then heads southeast, skirting Calver Hill, onto a road at Thirns, before climbing again to regain the contour.

Finally a walled path is joined which leads down to the attractive village of Reeth.

Looking down North Hush with Gorton, Friarfold and Bunton Hush directly across the valley (top).

Gunnerside Gill and the ruins of Blakethwaite Smelt Mill (centre).

Gunnerside, along the "royal road" through Swaledale beside the river (right).

Section 8: **Reeth to Richmond**

10.9 miles (*17.5 km*)

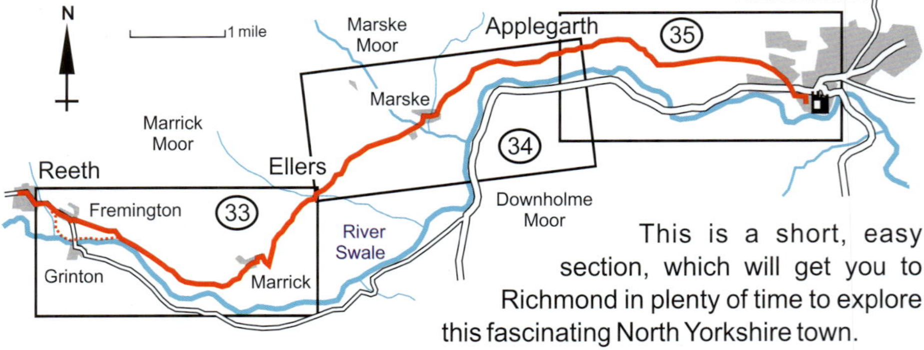

This is a short, easy section, which will get you to Richmond in plenty of time to explore this fascinating North Yorkshire town.

Reeth, *the 'capital' of upper Swaledale*, sits high up on the hillside overlooking the confluence of the River Swale and Arkle Beck. The large village green, surrounded by several pubs and hotels, makes a fine spot to sit and enjoy the views across the valley, and is the point where the two routes from the previous section meet.

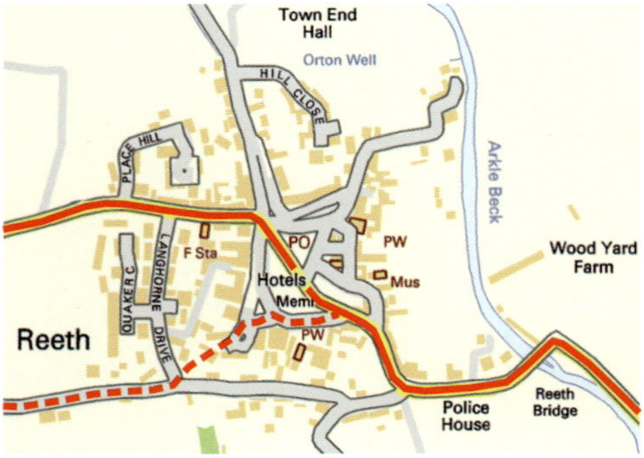

Reeth is closely linked to Grinton, down by the river, where the parish church is located. The youth hostel sits high above at Grinton Lodge.

Reeth flourished in the heyday of lead mining, and the history of the industry can be found at the Swaledale Museum, housed in the old Methodist School.

Reeth

From the village green, head down the main road for Richmond, to cross Arkle Beck at Reeth Bridge. The road runs alongside the beck for 150 metres, before it curves away for Fremington. At this point there's the opportunity to take a popular riverside path which avoids ¾ of a mile of road walking.

Otherwise, continue through Fremington, taking the Marske byroad on the left where the main road curves south.

Just under half a mile further on at a fork, take the narrow lane on the right to Marrick Priory. The priory was founded for Benedictine nuns in 1154 and is now used as an outdoor education centre.

A gate on the left leads up through woods on the flagged Nunnery Steps and into Marrick. The road leads through the hamlet, curving round at the second T-junction behind the old school house to join a footpath northeast crossing fields to the isolated farmhouse at Ellers.

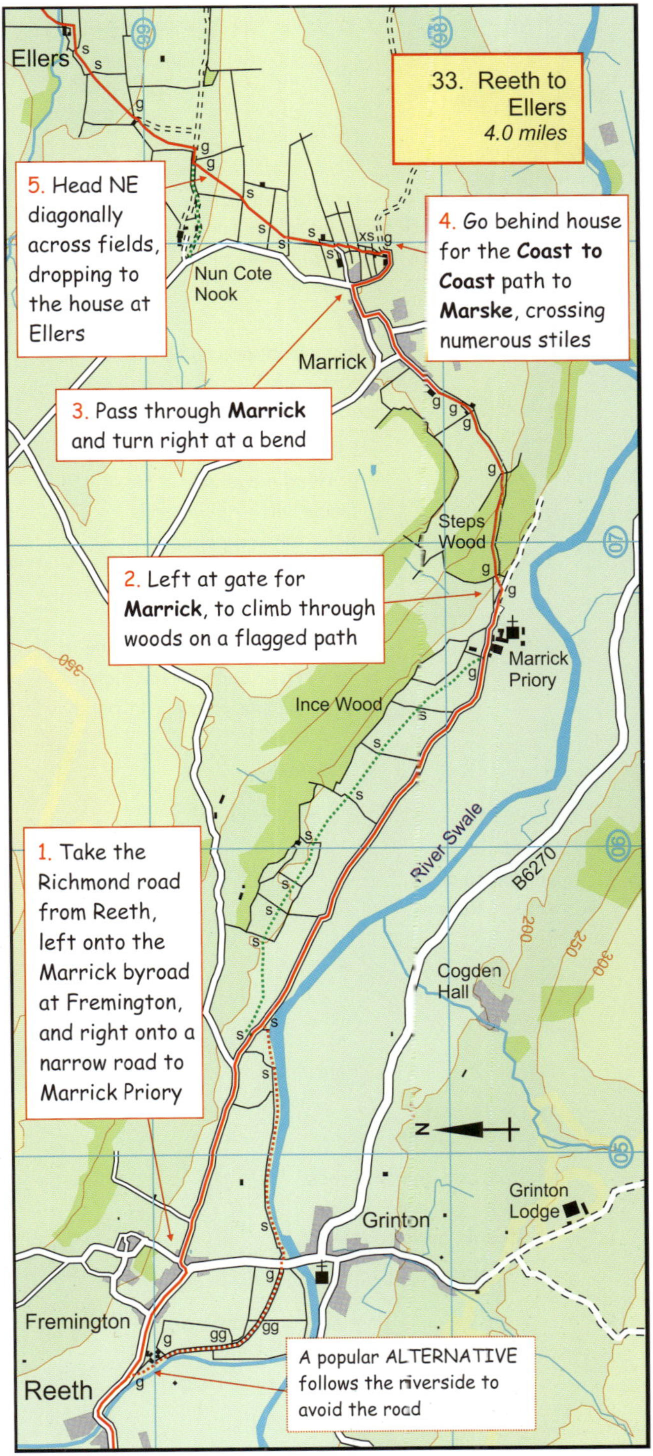

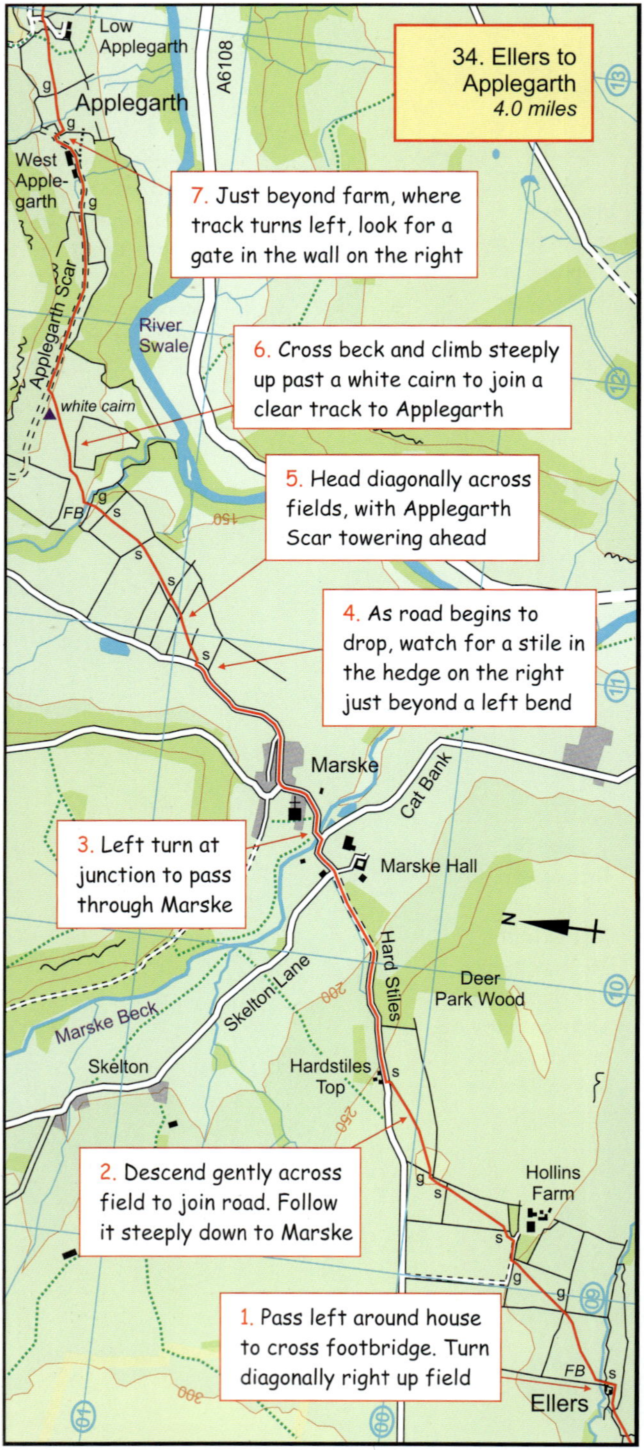

Church of St Edmund, Marske

Go around the house to cross a footbridge, then head diagonally uphill across fields, past Hollins Farm to the hill top. A diagonal path across a long field now leads down to a wallstile and out onto the road, which descends steeply to Marske.

Follow the road climbing NE through the village and take a stile on the right as the road begins to descend again to cross fields and Clapgate Beck before climbing steeply up to Applegarth Scar, where a white stone cairn marks the junction of a farm track to West Applegarth.

Beyond West Applegarth turn right through a gate to follow the bridleway across fields heading east, joining another farm track briefly at East Applegarth before cutting left through a gate. The path curves gently beneath Whitcliffe Scar.

Willance's Leap is the spot where, whilst hunting in thick fog in 1606, Robert Willance plunged with his horse from the high cliffs. Amazingly he survived. He managed to stay alive through the depths of a bitterly cold winter's night by putting his shattered leg inside the carcass of his dead horse, until rescued the next day

Further along, the embankment walling of a fort can be seen. Classified by the Royal Commission for the Historic Monuments of England as a Romano-British fort, it has never been excavated and so may be pre-Roman in origin, dating from the Iron Age or the Bronze Age.

The path now passes through Whitecliff Wood and on to join the road at High Leases, which leads directly down into Richmond.

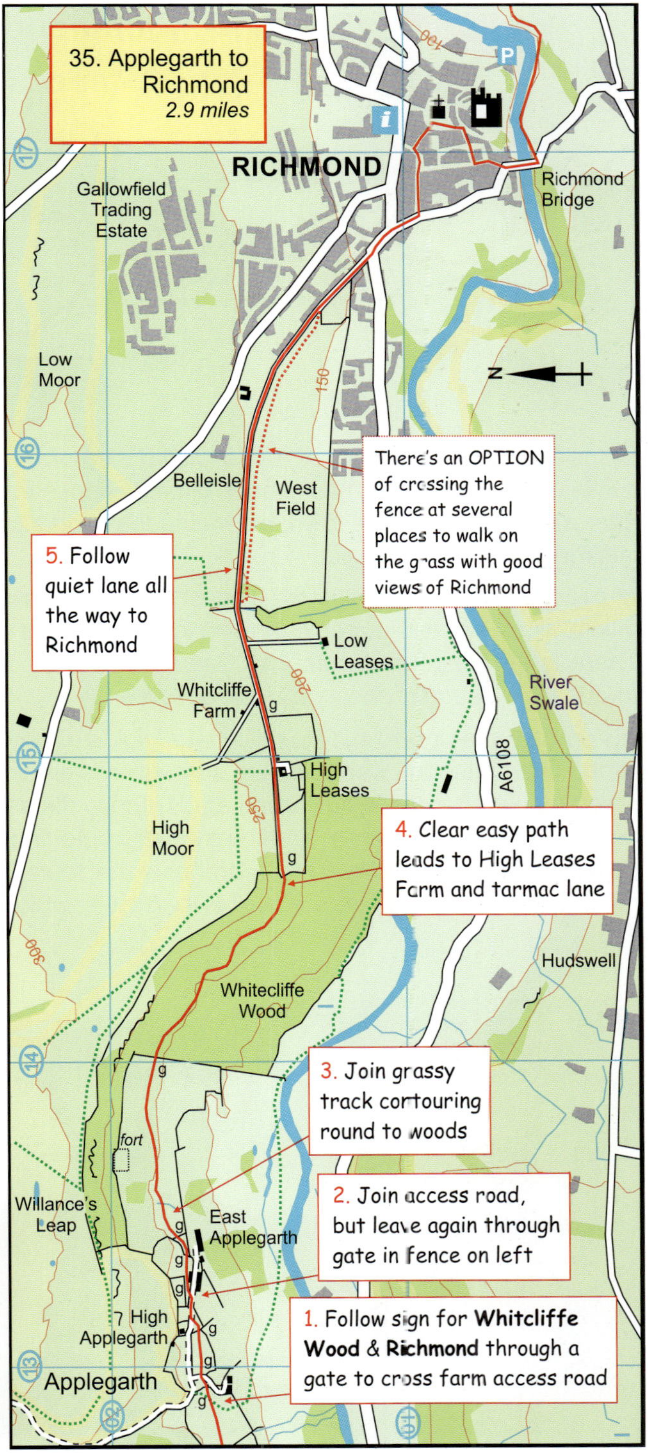

Section 9: **Richmond to Ingleby Cross**

23.2 miles (*37.3 km*)

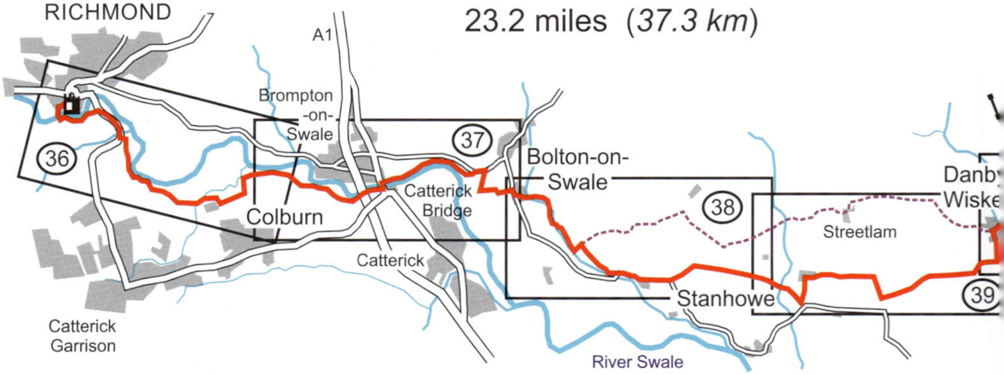

Some Coast to Coast walkers take a full day's break in Richmond, to explore all that this historic market town has to offer. Others choose to press on to Catterick Bridge after a quick break in the town, extending the short section from Reeth and cutting into the next section to Ingleby Cross.

At over 23 miles this is by far the longest section of the whole walk, and the flattest – mile after mile of fertile arable farming land stretching across the Vale of Mowbray. There is the option to break it at Danby Wiske, but Wainwright preferred to get through this *slough of despond* in one go.

His original attempts to stick to designated rights of way across fields were thwarted by the fact that many were blocked, through design or disuse, so he was forced to revert for over 8 miles to quiet rural roads. Today things have changed, walkers are now welcomed to the area, and the modern route finds its way happily along field edges and grassy tracks. This is probably the route Wainwright originally had in mind, though many walkers still use his road route, which is shorter and quicker.

Richmond

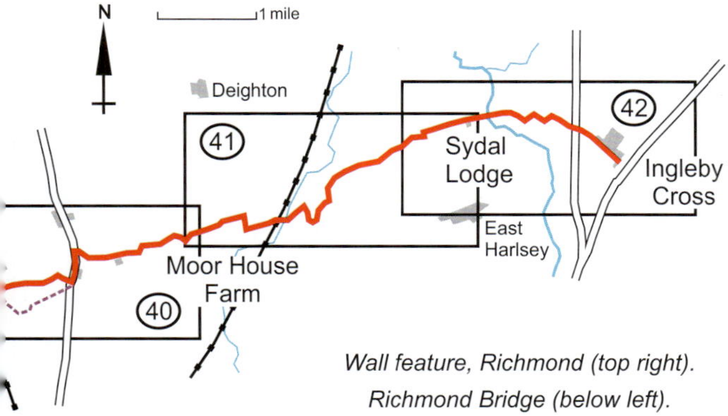

Wall feature, Richmond (top right).
Richmond Bridge (below left).
Holy Trinity Church, Market Square (right).
The River Swale at Richmond (bottom).

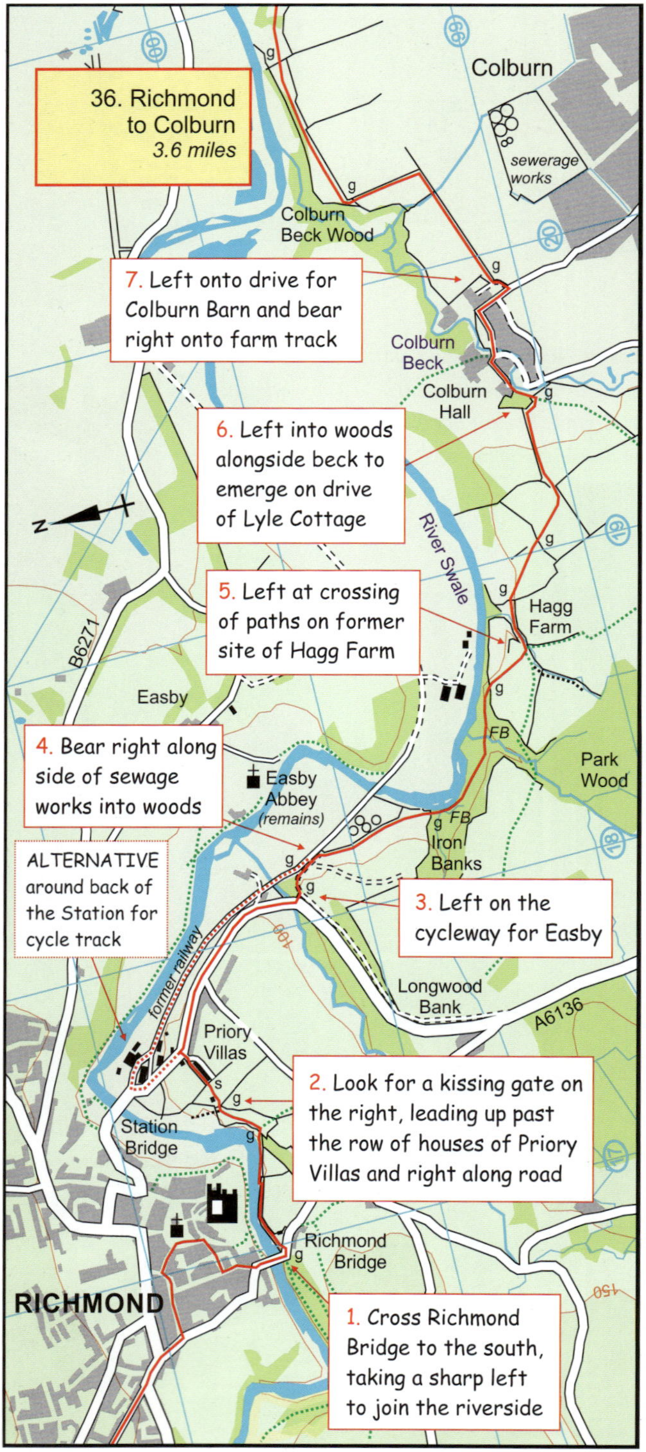

Castle walls above the Swale

Make your way from the market place through narrow streets down to Richmond Bridge. Once across turn sharp left to join a pleasant riverside path, eventually bearing away, right, to pass between farm buildings and past a row of houses - Priory Villas. Either turn right along the main road, cutting left onto a cycleway, or bear left to pass behind the Station and join the cycleway there. Cut right to pass the sewage works into quiet woodland.

Beyond the woods the way turns left at the former site of Hagg Farm, before climbing diagonally southeast across fields, curving left at the brow to follow a field hedge down to Colburn. Here a left turn through trees besides a beck brings you out onto the road.

Pass through the quiet hamlet, turning south along the road and left onto the drive of Colburn Barn. The path continues east, along farm tracks, above Colburn Beck Wood and the River Swale.

The path now bears away from the river to St. Giles Farm, where it joins the access road for a brief moment before a gate on the left leads onto a lofty enclosed way, with the Swale far below to the left.

The track cuts downhill to pass under the busy A1, another milestone, this one marking two thirds of the walk completed.

Pass under the old railway bridge, then curve right to cross it, returning to the riverside on the northern bank. The way continues steadily eastwards, eventually being pushed uphill onto a bridle path beside the busy B6271. A right and a left take you on quiet lanes into Bolton-on-Swale.

Take time to visit the Jenkins Memorial in St Mary's churchyard. It commemorates Henry Jenkins, born 1500, died 1670, aged 169.

Jenkins Memorial

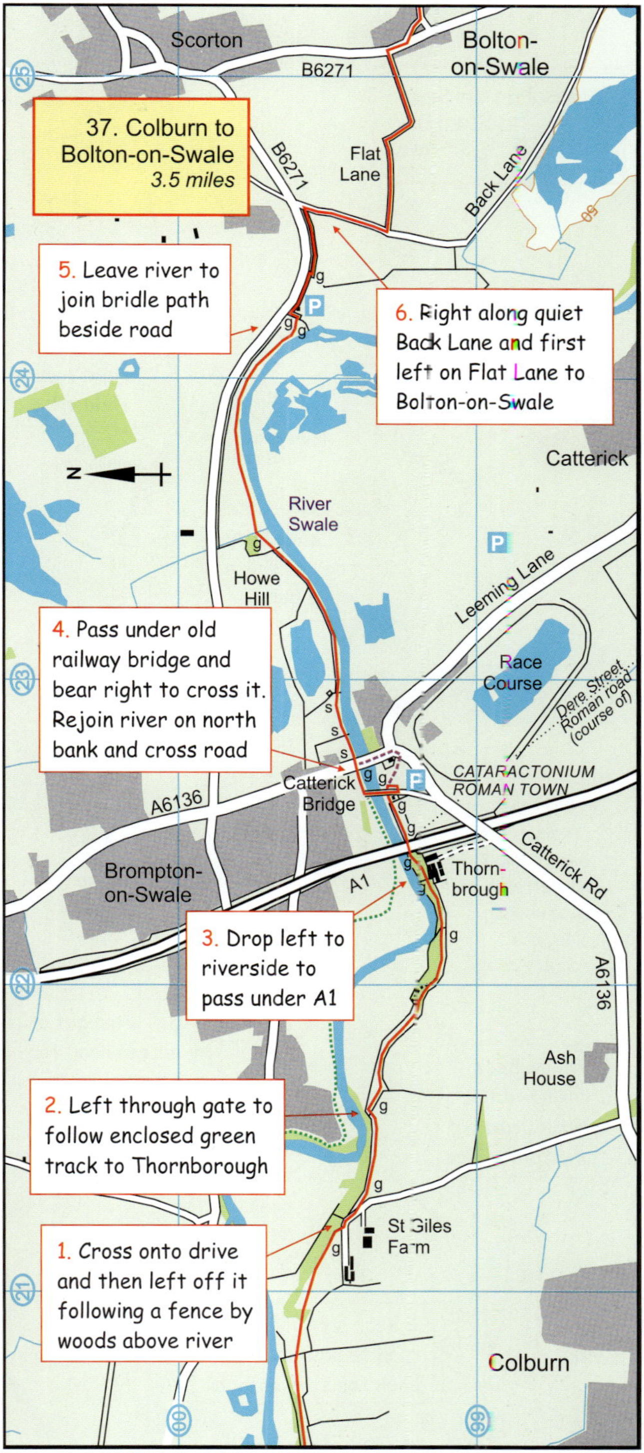

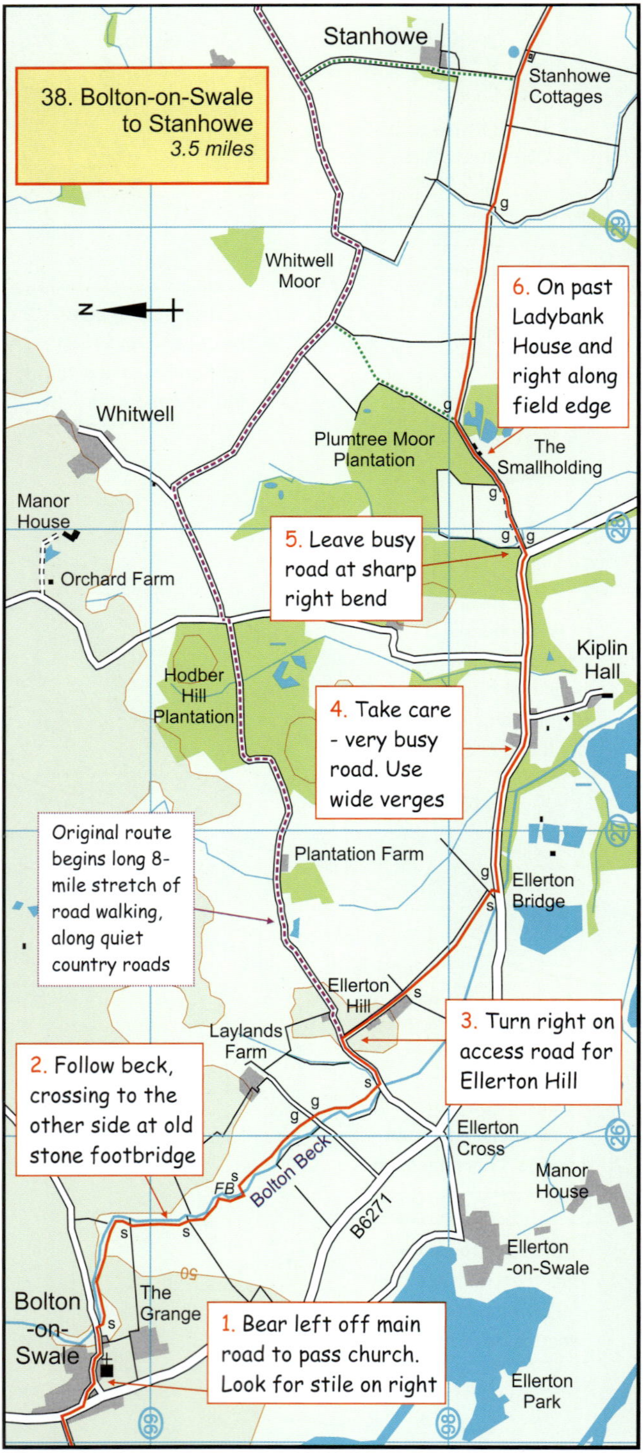

Kiplin Hall

Take the side road past St Mary's church and cross a stile to follow Bolton Beck towards Ellerton Hill. Here the modern route leaves the quiet road and heads southeast for Ellerton Bridge, and a brief spell along the busy B6271.

If you're lucky Kiplin Hall may be open and offering refreshments. Built as a hunting lodge in the 1620s by George Calvert, secretary of state to King James I, it is now run by a trust and open to the public.

The path leaves the road at a corner, passing Ladybank House with its delightful garden carvings, before turning east again along arable field hedges to the ruined Stanhowe Cottages.

The path continues along hedgerows to touch the B6271 once more, but a left turn takes you past Red House and up the access road for Moor House. Skirt the farm buildings to the right and continue east across fields, taking care after a rickety footbridge to keep right along the hedge, passing through a gap which takes you along the other side out to the road opposite Brockholme.

Turn right, then left to pass High Brockholme. The way continues along field hedges and an enclosed track, eventually leading to another road which takes you into Danby Wiske.

The White Swan at Danby Wiske is a welcome sight. Many walkers break this section here, which just happens to be the lowest point on the Coast to Coast path between the shores.

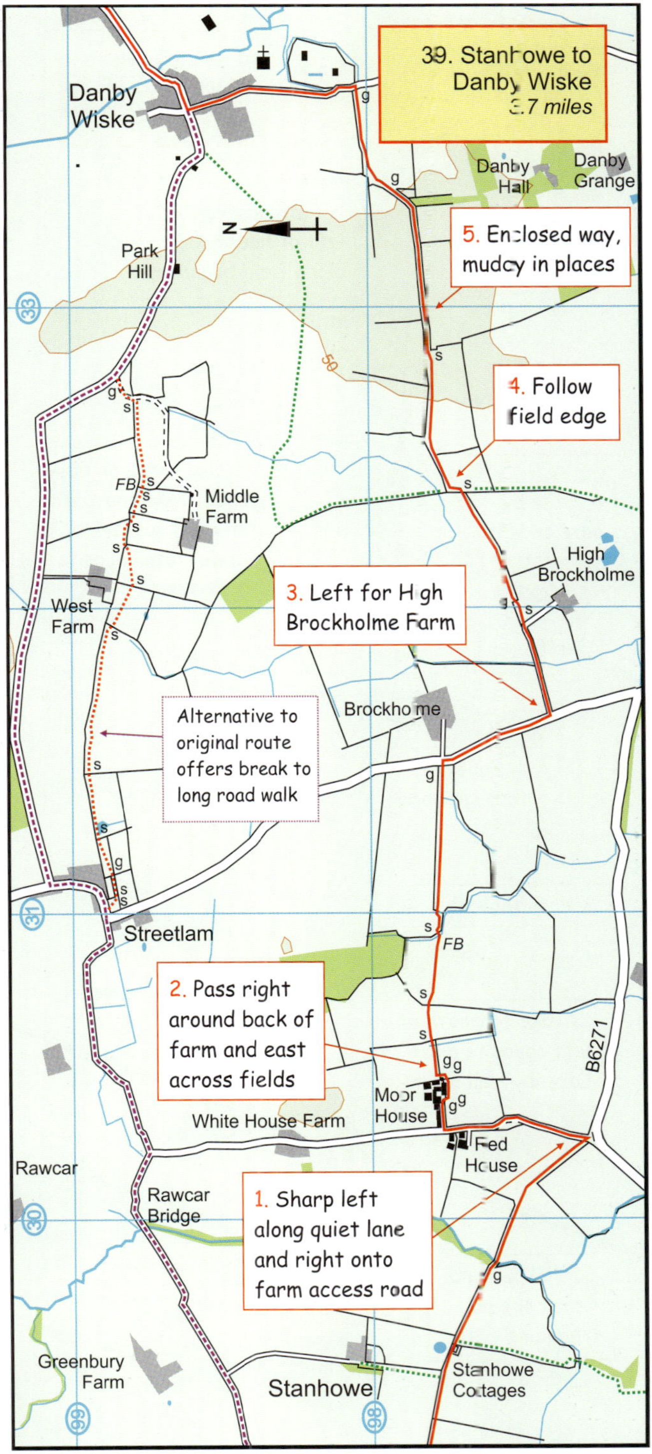

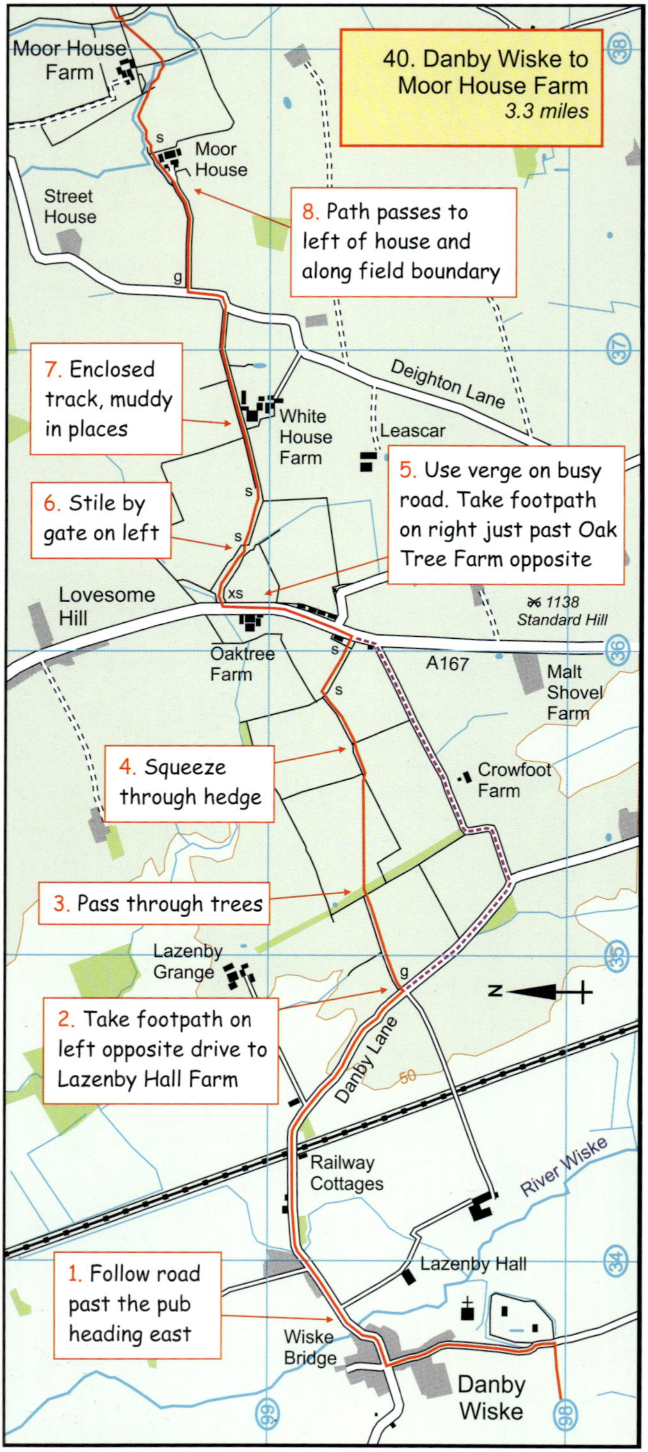

Take the road past the pub heading east and up over the railway. A footpath on the left leads east across fields to the A167.

Nearby was fought the Battle of the Standard in 1138. An invading Scottish army was met by an English army hastily organised by the Archbishop of York. 6,000 Galloway Picts led the Scottish attack, but being unprotected by any armour, were cut down under an onslaught of English arrows. The Scots King David escaped, but as many as 10,000 Scots were slaughtered that day.

The way leaves the road opposite Oaktree Farm to continue east, past White House Farm, crossing Deighton Lane and on past Moor House.

The path shadows a beck to pass to the right of Moor House Farm, crossing back diagonally over a field to a footbridge, and on up to the farm at Northfield House.

Follow the access road down to the road and go right, taking a left up to Wray House. The path crosses two stiles and curves behind the house to a railway crossing, where some care is needed.

Once safely over, head for a stile and footbridge opposite. A gate leads right alongside a hedge to a gap on the right, where another hedge on the left leads out to the road.

Easy walking now, with increasingly tantalising views of the Cleveland Hills ahead, as the tarmac road runs on for some way, past Harsley Grove and Deepdale. Turn right at the first T-junction, and left at the next, to join the access road up to Sydal Lodge.

Keep left past the farm buildings and across a stile.

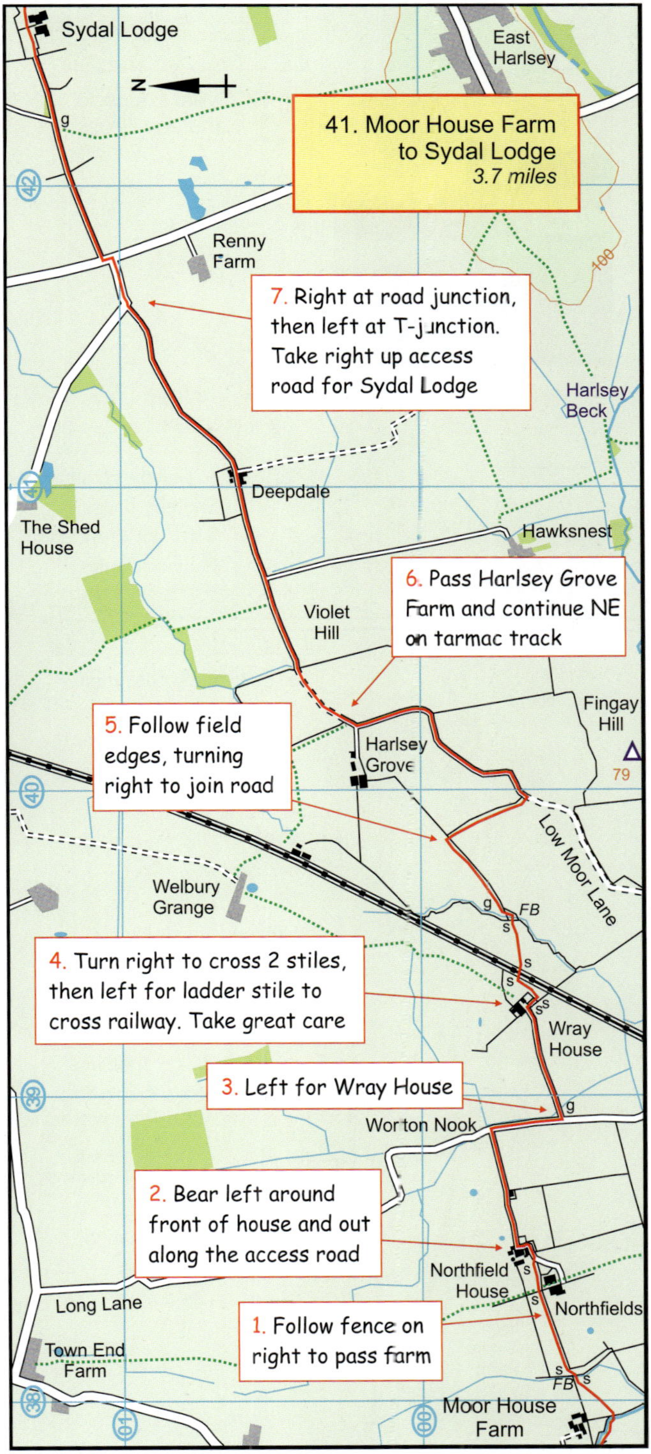

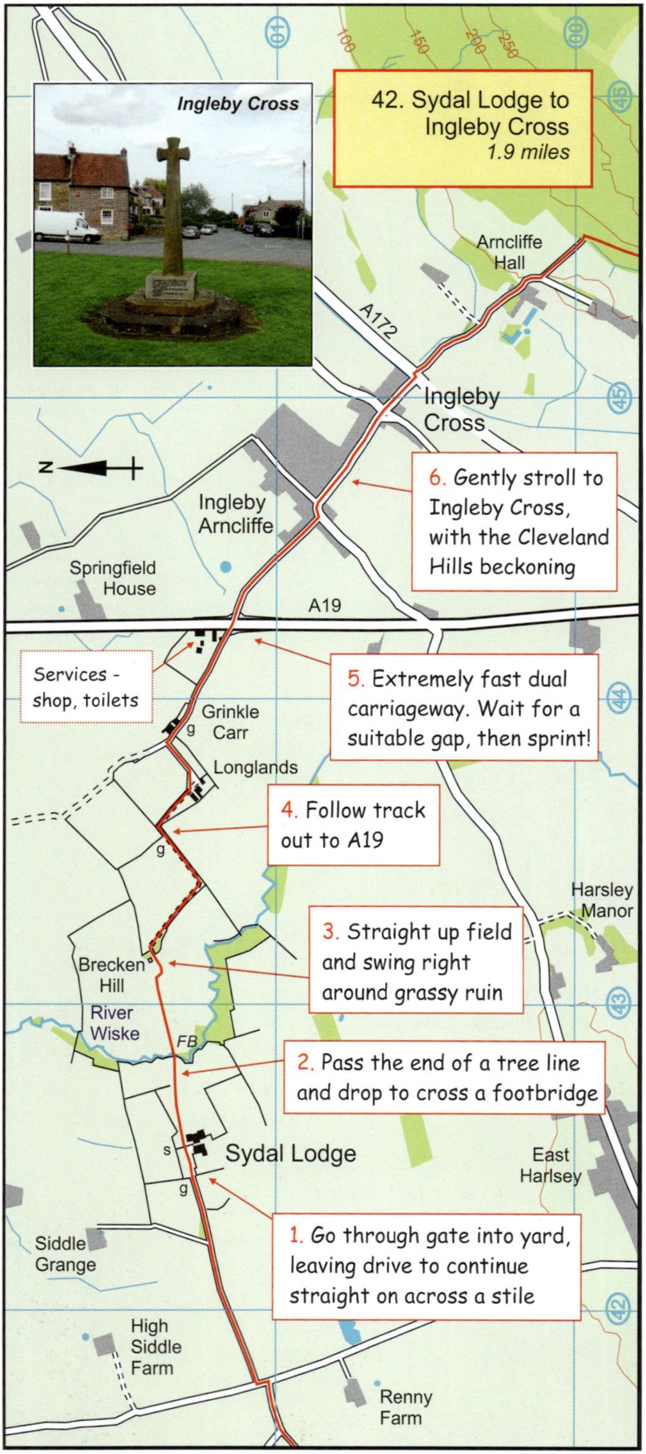

The path crosses to the right of a line of trees, down to a footbridge, then straight up the other side to pass right by a grassy ruin at Brecken Hill, which stood complete when Wainwright first sketched it.

The path leads unmistakeably down, on a zigzag course, past Longlands and Cringle Carr to the very busy A19, which must be crossed somehow.

The quiet road opposite leads to Ingleby Arncliffe, where a quick left and right take you on down to Ingleby Cross and the Blue Bell Inn.

If you stayed over at Danby Wiske and arrive in good time, consider visiting nearby Mount Grace Priory, the ruins of a 14th century Carthusian priory.

If you walked all 23 miles from Richmond, then head straight for the pub and collapse there.

Mount Grace Priory

Section 10: **Ingleby Cross to Clay Bank Top**

11.6 miles (*18.7 km*)

At last, it's back to the hills for the final stage of your journey; the North York Moors National Park will now see you all the way to the east coast. In good weather this is an excellent day's walk along the steep escarpment of the Cleveland Hills, with fine long views north over the Cleveland plains.

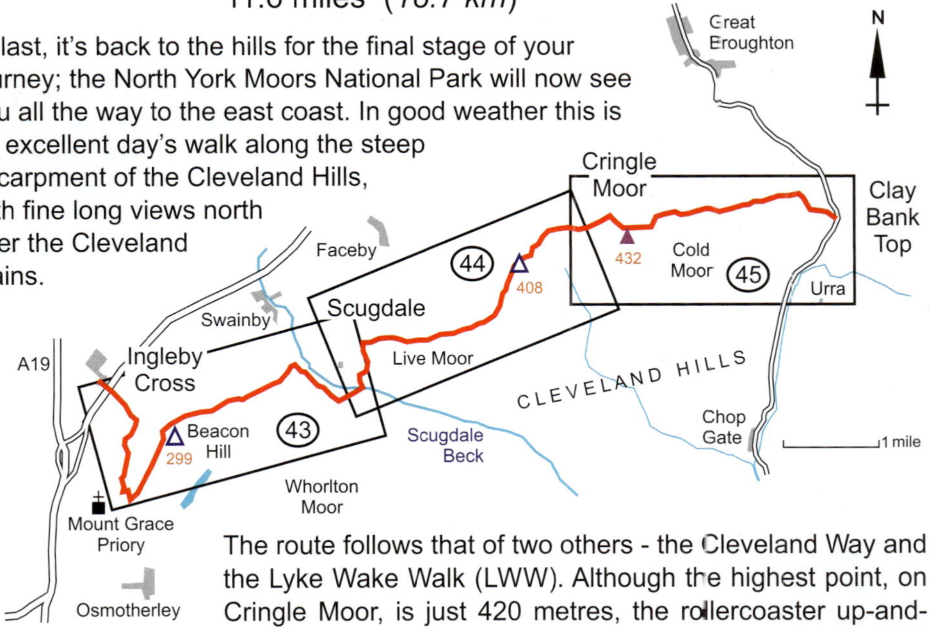

The route follows that of two others - the Cleveland Way and the Lyke Wake Walk (LWW). Although the highest point, on Cringle Moor, is just 420 metres, the rollercoaster up-and-down nature of the walking gives a total ascent of over 1000 metres. It's only 12 miles in distance, but you will be tired by the end. At Clay Bank Top there's nothing but a nearby carpark with a view. Accommodation must be sought north or south, over a mile by road - the next en route is 9 miles away at the Lion Inn.

Descending from Carlton Moor for Cringle Moor

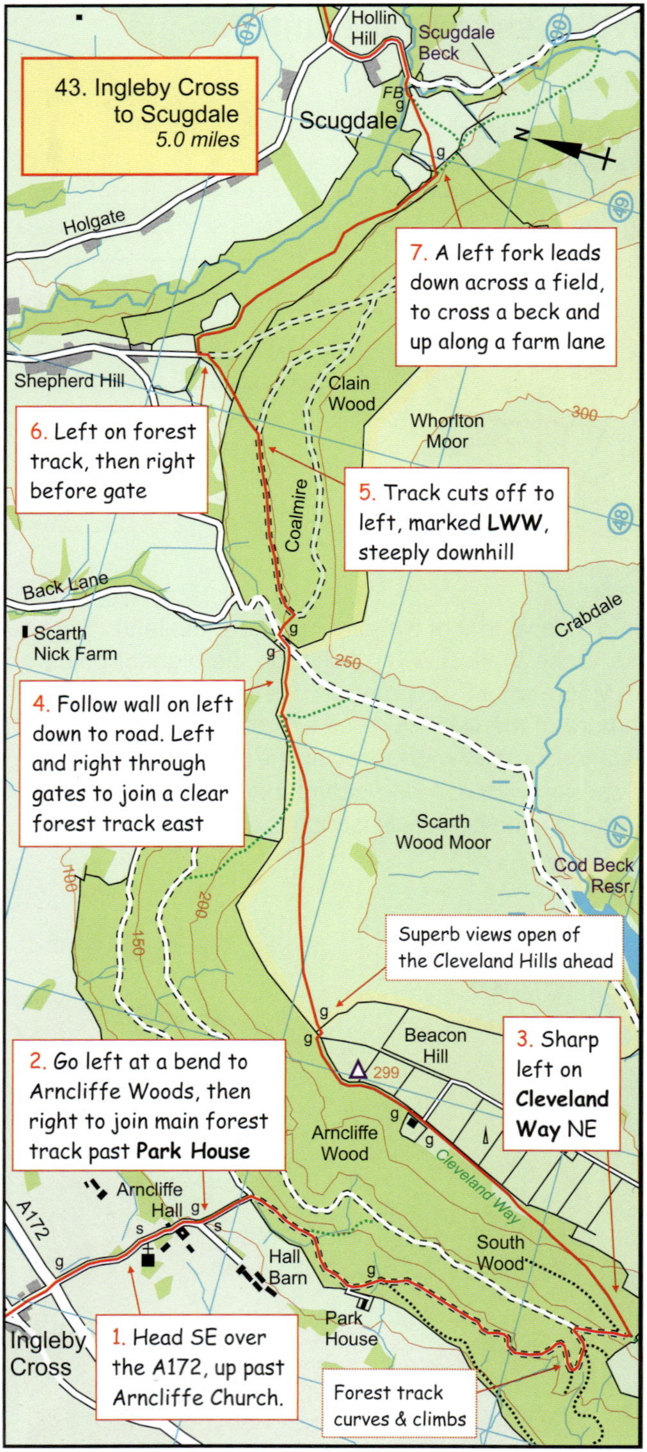

Arncliffe Hall

From Ingleby Cross set off southeast, past the Bluebell Inn, towards the wooded hills. Cross the busy A172 and on up the lane past the church and Arncliffe Hall, bearing left through a gate for **Park House**. Once into the woods, turn right and follow the forest track which eventually zigzags steeply uphill to join the **Cleveland Way** by a gate. A right turn here takes you to Osmotherley, a sharp left on towards Robin Hood's Bay. The tree-lined path climbs uphill, past a radio transmission station onto Beacon Hill, and the first sight of the Cleveland Hills.

The path crosses Scarth Wood Moor and drops into more woods at Coalmire. The path eventually leaves the forest track for a steep downhill section marked **LWW** on a boulder, with a nearby marker to that walk's creator, Bill Cowley. A sharp right off the main track leads onto a pleasant woodland track, then left across a field to cross Scugdale Beck.

Across Scugdale Beck the lane leads up past a farm to the road at Huthwaite Green. Across the road a bench makes a nice resting point before the next climb.

Take the bridlegate by the bench, signed **Cleveland Way**, and follow the path as it skirts the edge of the woods. At a corner with two gates, take the one, right, which leads up into the woods and on to Live Moor.

A flagged path takes you up to the cairn at the summit, with grand panoramic views. The sharp edge of Carlton Moor is dominant ahead, with the unique outline of Roseberry Topping in the distance beyond.

The clear path follows the escarpment edge, past the former site of the Carlton Moor gliding club. The club buildings have now been removed and the runway is being reseeded. Beyond the trig point a steep descent (the first of many) winds its way down around the remains of a former alum mine. Cross the road to pass the nearby café and camping site, before the climb up to Cringle Moor.

Top of Carlton Moor

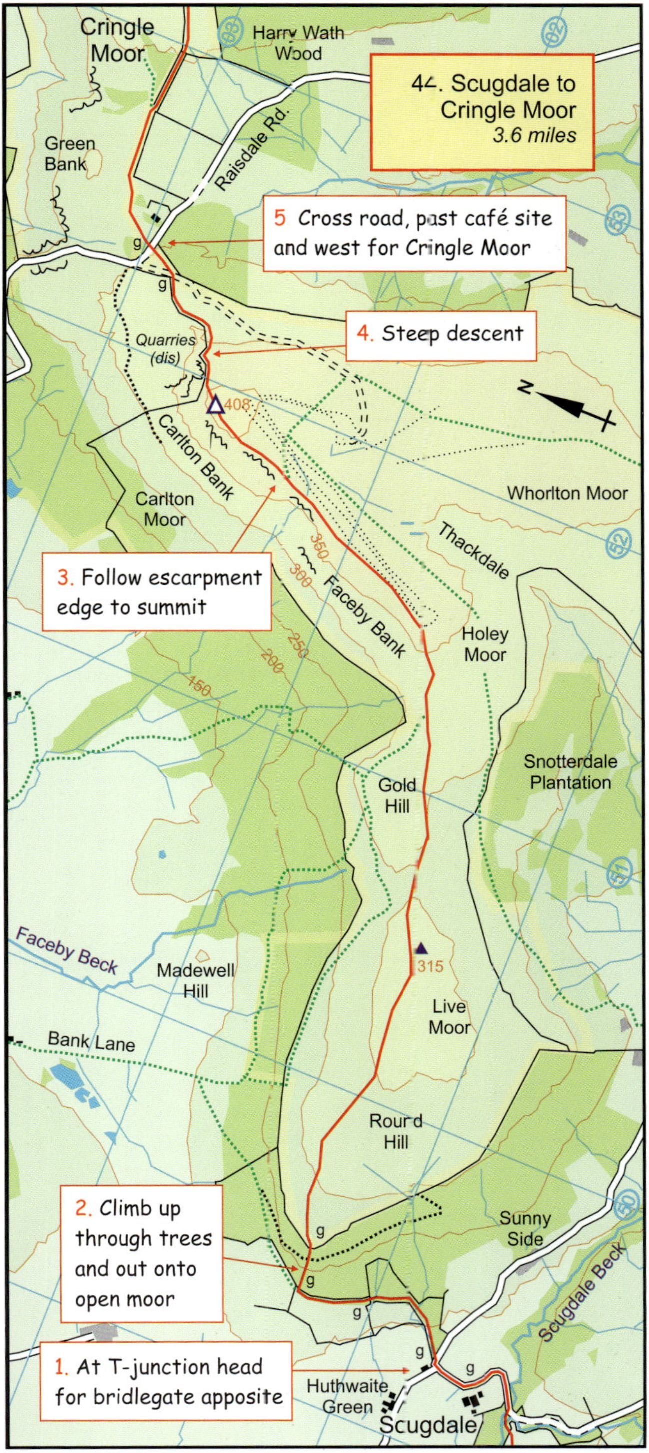

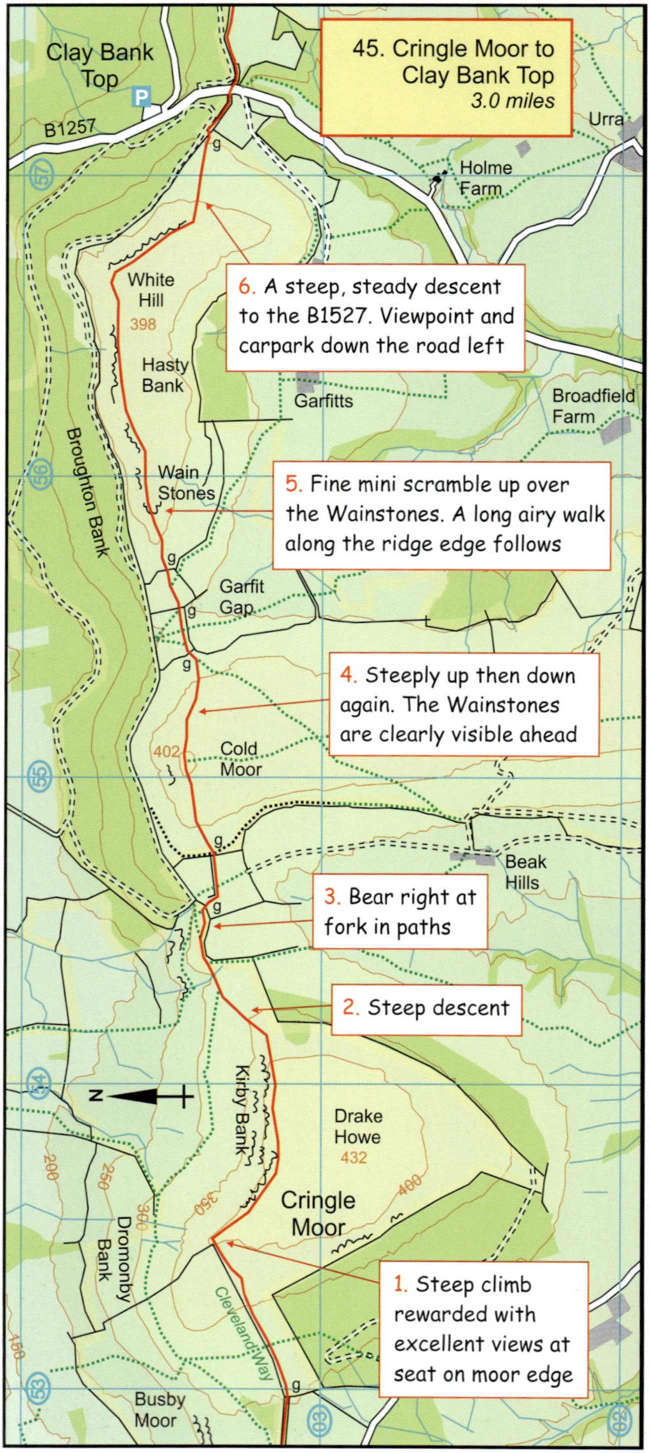

More stone paving leads uphill to the rocky promontory at Cringle End. This is a fine viewpoint, and well worth a sit down on the stone bench provided - a memorial to Alan Falconer who devised the Cleveland Way. The second of the great national trails, the Cleveland Way runs 100 miles around the rim of the North York Moors and the North Sea coast from Helmsley to Filey. It was finally opened in 1969, a year after Falconer died.

The path continues, skirting the edge above Kirby Bank. The summit here is some distance away in the heather to the south, at Drake Howe, where a Bronze Age burial mound marks the spot.

Another steep descent and up again over Cold Moor. The final down-and-up beyond leads onto Hasty Bank and the delightful Wainstones. Another place to rest and look back over Cold and Cringle Moors,

A fine cliff edge level track now leads along Hasty Bank, before the last steep descent of the day to Clay Bank Top.

Onto Scarth Wood Moor from Beacon Hill - first view of the Cleveland Hills ahead (top).

Cringle Moor (above left).

Cold Moor from the Wainstones (right).

Across Clay Bank Top from Hasty Bank (below).

Section 11: **Clay Bank Top to Glaisdale**

18.5 miles (*29.8 km*)

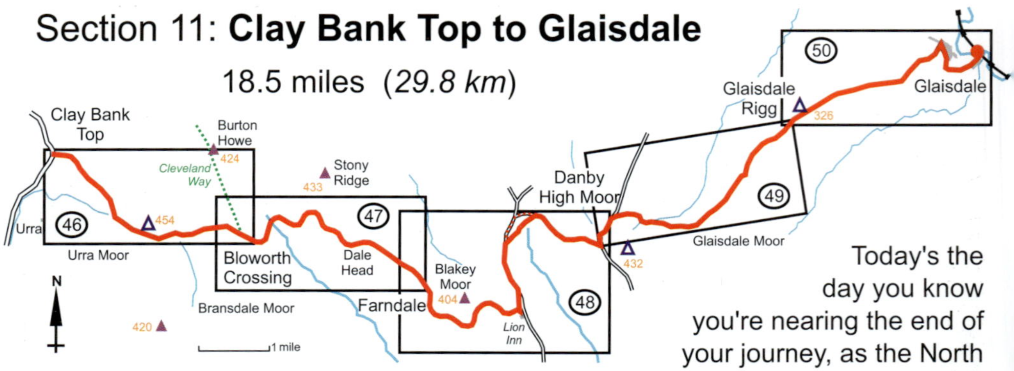

Today's the day you know you're nearing the end of your journey, as the North Sea edges prominently into view when you cross Danby High Moor.

It's quite a long section, at almost 19 miles, but after the first steady climb from Clay Bank Top to Urra Moor it's level, fast-paced walking all the way.

Some people choose to split the final two days into three, with breaks at the Lion Inn on Blakey Ridge, and at Grosmont.

This is rich heather moorland, managed for grouse shooting, but bearing also the scars of the former iron mining industry around Rosedale. The Rosedale Ironstone Railway was constructed in the mid nineteenth century to carry the iron ore northwards, linking onto Teesdale and Durham. The railway was finally closed and dismantled in 1929 with the decline of ironstone production, but the trackbed remains as a very elegant and useful way for moorland walkers.

There is only one habitation between Clay Bank Top and Glaisdale, and that is the Lion Inn at Blakey Ridge. This is an oasis at which almost all walkers will want to stop, even if only for a short break before continuing onwards.

The Lion Inn comes into view

Hand Stone

Cross the B1257 to Hagg's Gate opposite, for the steady climb along a paved path up to Carr Ridge where the way levels out. It's easy walking all the way now, with just a slight gentle rise to the highest point along the Cleveland Hills at the trig point on Round Hill.

Here you pass the Hand Stone, and a little further on the Face Stone.

Keep along the clear main track until it bends sharply left. Here continue straight on along a faint path over wet ground, to join the old Rosedale Ironstone Railway track heading southeast.

Face Stone

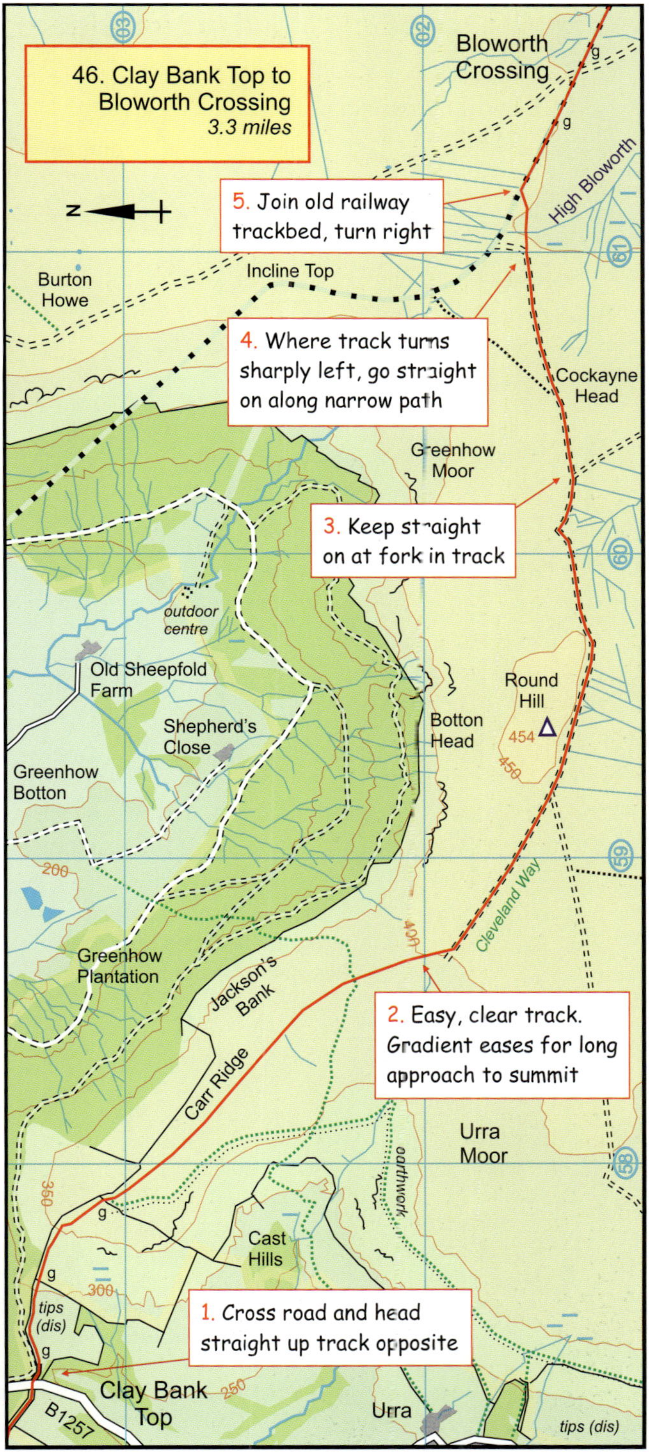

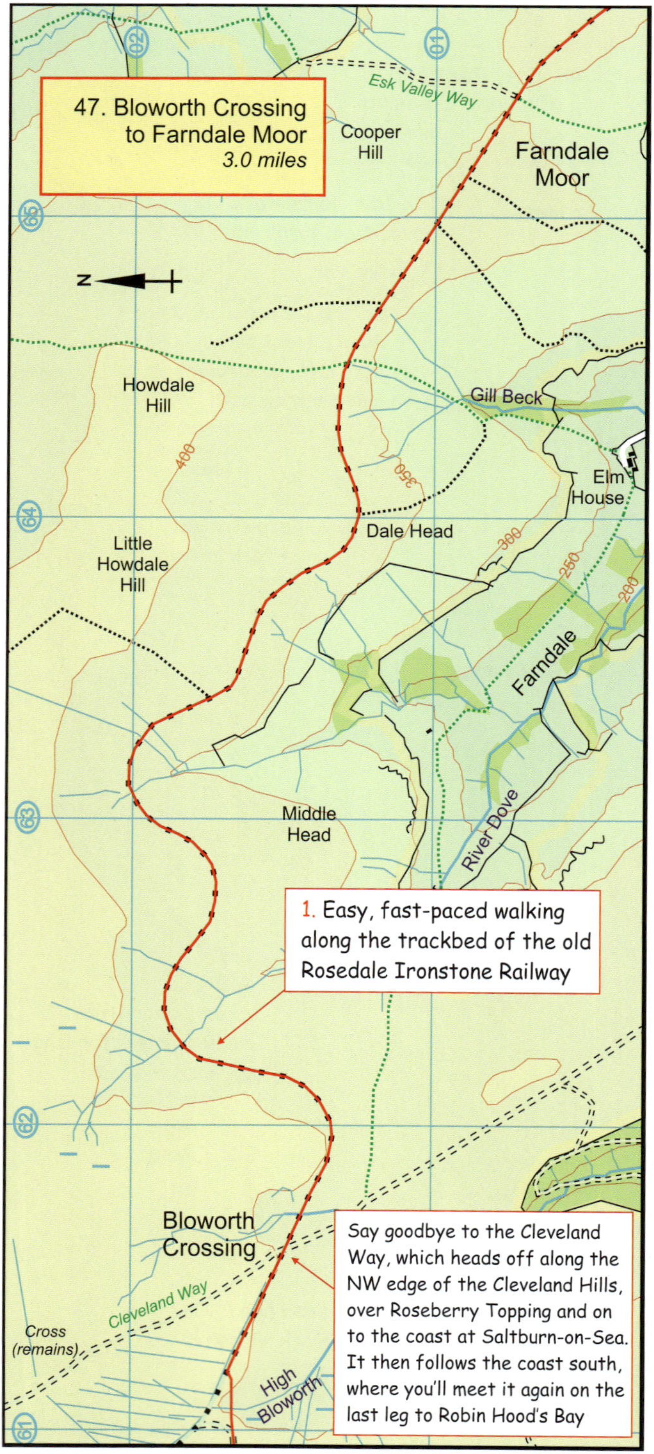

A rough moor road crosses at Bloworth Crossing, taking the Cleveland Way northwest. Continue along the railway track south east, as it curves, dead level, along embankments and cuttings, following the contour of the moors' southern edge. No problems route finding and a fast pace is picked up.

Farndale opens up below to the right, and Westerdale to the left, where the Esk Valley Way joins.

As you round a curve at High Blakey Moor, the 400 year old Lion Inn comes into view across the valley on Blakey Ridge. The path eventually leaves the railway track to head up, past a barn, to the pub by an ancient tumulus, Blakey Howe, at one time dug out to form a cock-fighting pit.

From here the way continues along the road north, to turn east at a junction near Young Ralph Cross, then north again onto High Danby Moor. A corner can be cut along a waymarked bridleway, emerging onto the road again by Fat Betty.

Young Ralph

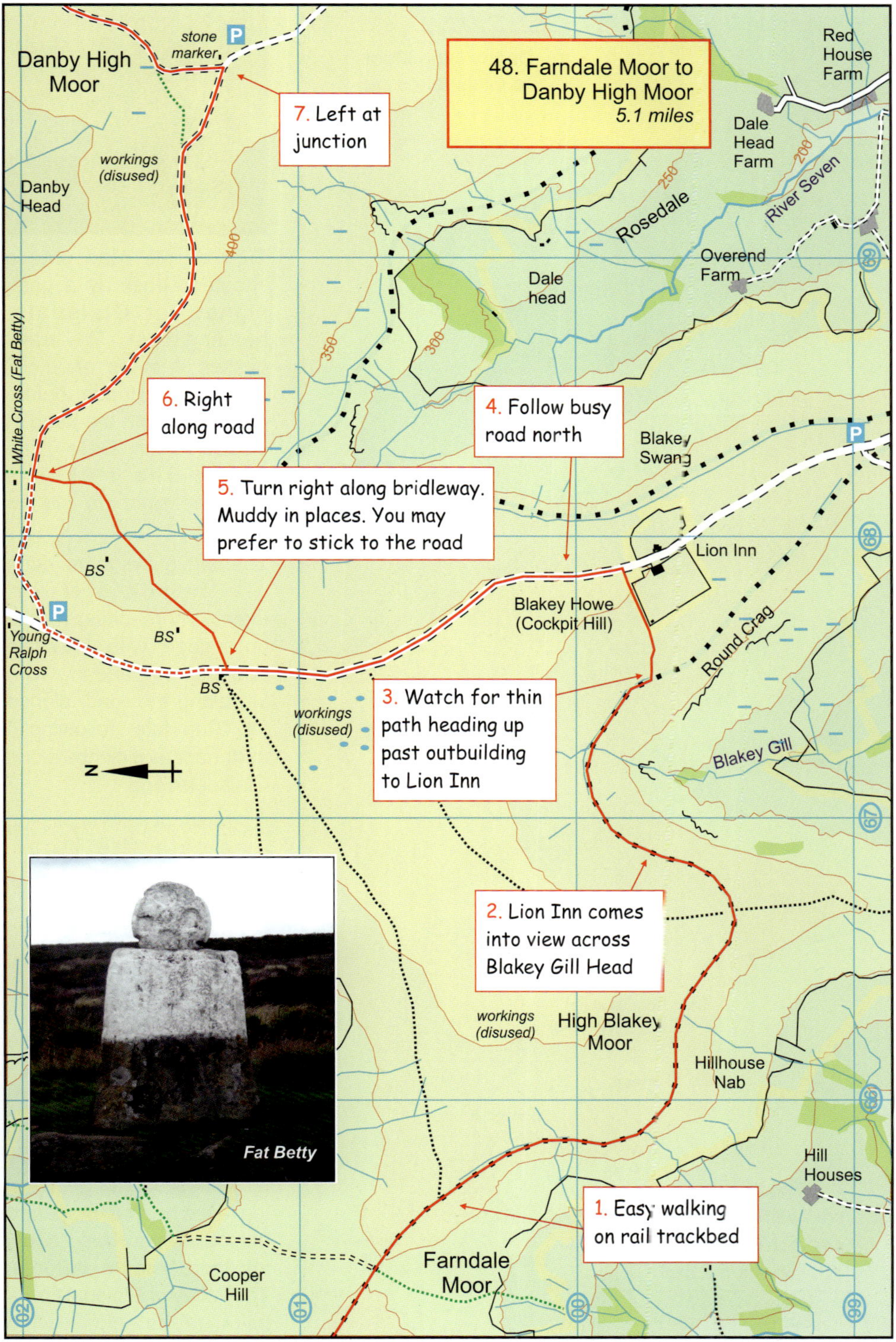
48. Farndale Moor to Danby High Moor
5.1 miles
1. Easy walking on rail trackbed
2. Lion Inn comes into view across Blakey Gill Head
3. Watch for thin path heading up past outbuilding to Lion Inn
4. Follow busy road north
5. Turn right along bridleway. Muddy in places. You may prefer to stick to the road
6. Right along road
7. Left at junction
Danby High Moor
stone marker
P
Danby Head
workings (disused)
White Cross (Fat Betty)
Red House Farm
Dale Head Farm
River Seven
Rosedale
Overend Farm
Dale head
Blakey Swang
Lion Inn
Blakey Howe (Cockpit Hill)
Round Crag
Blakey Gill
Young Ralph Cross
BS
High Blakey Moor
Hillhouse Nab
Hill Houses
Farndale Moor
Cooper Hill
400
350
300
250
200
Fat Betty

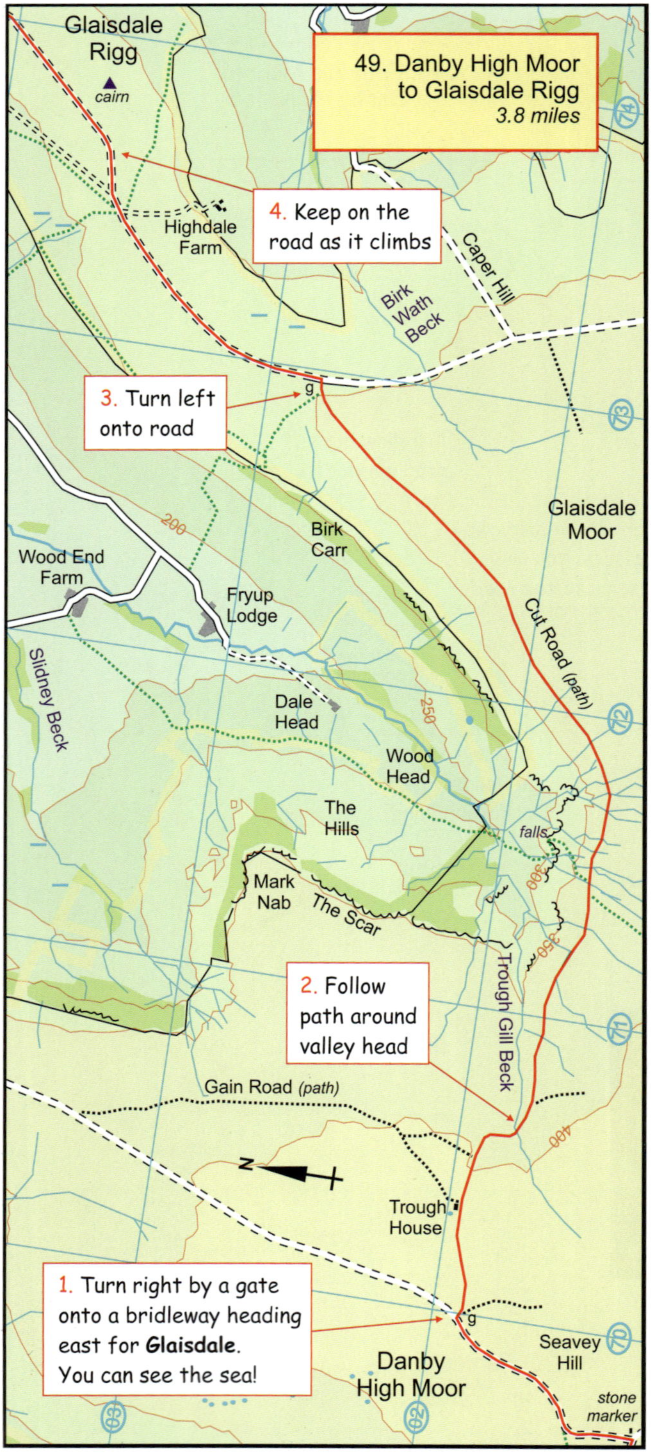

Trough House

Turn off the road onto a shooters' track by a gate, signed for **Glaisdale**, heading east. The track passes a stone shooters' hut, Trough House, before curving around the head of Great Fryup Dale. The North Sea makes a welcome sight on the far horizon.

The path sticks to the edge of Glaisdale Moor, eventually reaching a road on a ridge, with Glaisdale opening out ahead. Turn left along the road, signed for **Glaisdale**, following it northeast as it climbs along Glaisdale Rigg.

A prominent cairn is passed away on the right. Eventually, as the road levels out, it curves left, to pass the trig point. Here the way lies straight on, along an old unmade moor road, marked as *unsuitable for motor vehicles*. This is the old **Whitby Road**, as shown on a prominent stone marker further on.

This is another fine, airy walk, descending gently to leave the heather moorland behind as you head down into more verdant pastures. The valley of Glaisdale runs below to the right, leading

"Whitby Road"

into Eskdale, which will take you eastwards towards the North Sea.

The track finally becomes a tarmac lane at a gate. Follow it down into Glasidale, where a right turn is taken at the main road junction.

Glaisdale is strung out along the road, which drops south, then east to Glaisdale station.

A short cut presents itself just beyond the junction. Bear left to join a narrow path that heads steeply downhill, emerging on a back lane. Turn left and follow this downhill. Eventually the lane emerges onto the main road by the Arncliffe Arms and Glaisdale station.

Beggar's Bridge

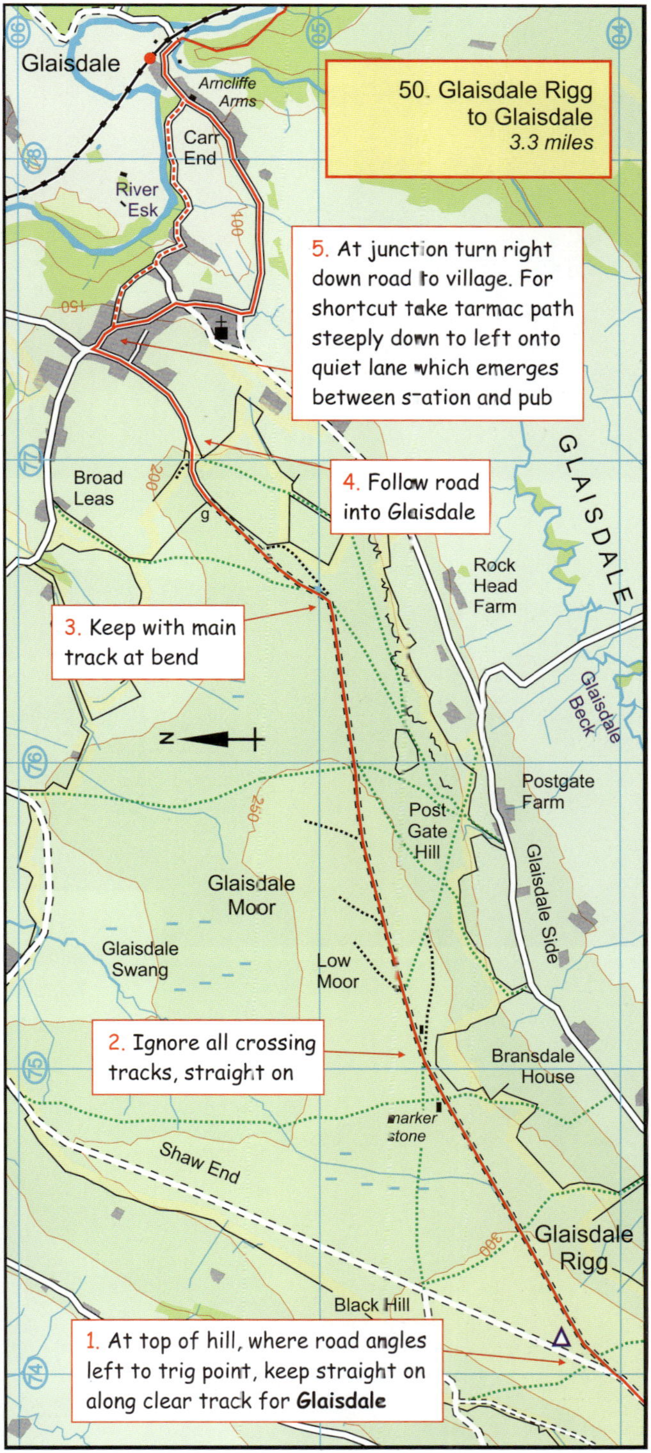

Climbing from Clay Bank Top for Urra Moor (top).
Heather moorland on Urra Moor (above).
The cliffs north of Ness Point (below).

Section 12: **Glaisdale to Robin Hood's Bay**

18.7 miles (*30.1 km*)

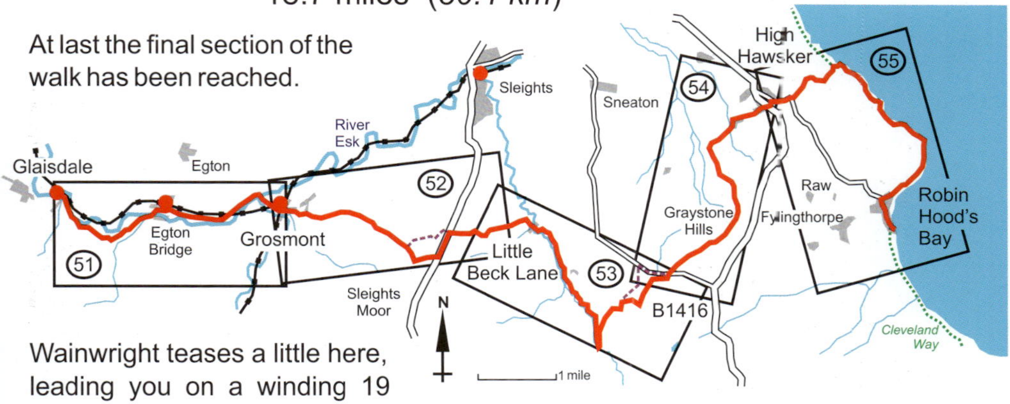

At last the final section of the walk has been reached.

Wainwright teases a little here, leading you on a winding 19 mile route which a crow could cover in under 11 miles. But there are plenty of rewards along the way: gentle riverside stretches, beautiful woodland, waterfalls, steam trains, open moorland, and finally a three mile clifftop walk along the North Sea coast which mirrors the start of your journey at St. Bees Head.

If you break this section at Grosmont, then you'll be sat in the Bay Hotel by mid-afternoon. Otherwise an early start is advisable, because the steam trains at Grosmont will undoubtedly delay you.

Some people choose to break this section at Hawsker, to enjoy a refreshed end to their Coast to Coast experience.

The cliff path beyond Maw Wyke Hole

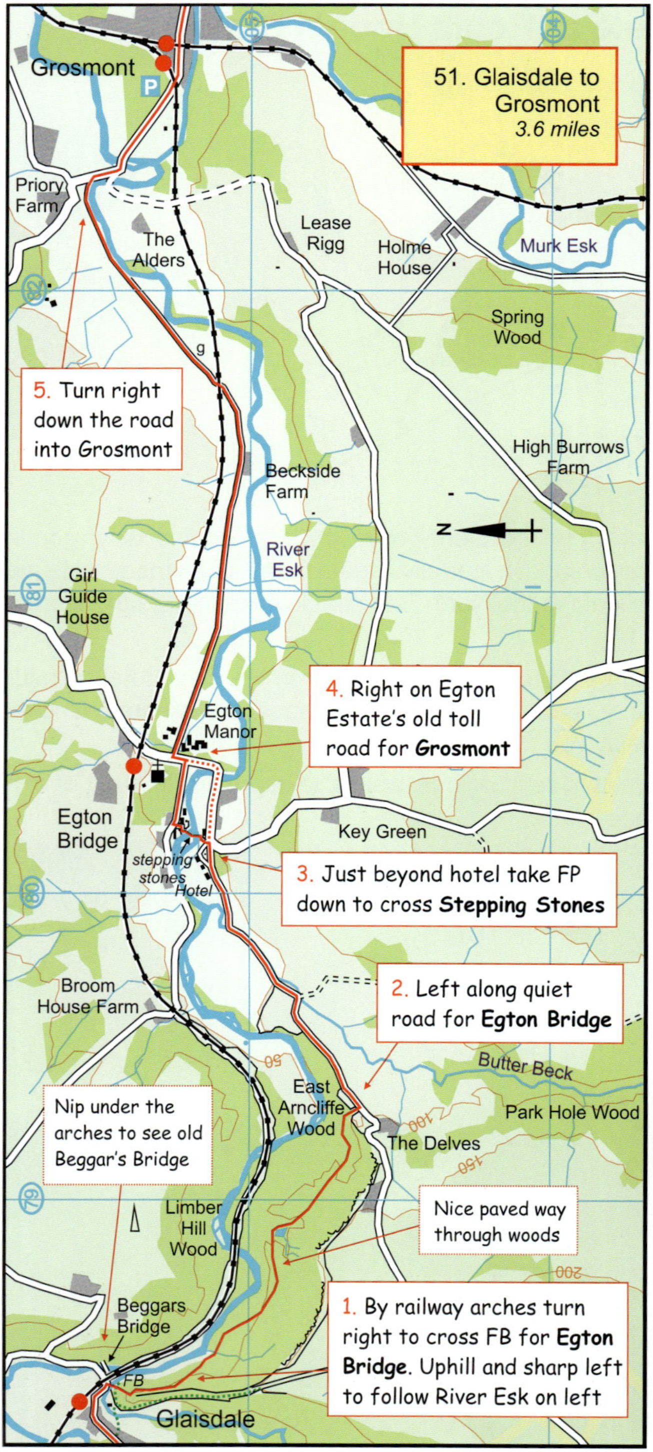

Head down the road by the station. The path cuts off to the right just by the railway arches, to cross the river at a footbridge, signed for **Egton Bridge**. But first take a moment to nip under the arches and see the old packhorse bridge.

The path climbs uphill, sharp left, to follow above the river along an old packhorse trail, flagged in places, through a lovely stretch of woodland. Emerge onto a quiet road, where a left turn takes you into the delightful village at Egton Bridge.

From here the old toll road leads through the Egton Manor Estate for **Grosmont**.

Grosmont lies on the junction of two railways: the mainline Esk Valley Railway links Middlesborough to Whitby, and the privately run North York Moors Railway which links to Pickering. The latter was saved from the Beeching cuts in 1965 by an enthusiastic group of volunteers, and the

Stepping stones, Egton Bridge

voluntary trust now runs regular steam trains along this beautiful moorland route. With careful planning and an overnight break here, you can indulge yourself with a 2½ hour round trip.

Eventually, though, you must return to the task at hand – cross the line and begin the long steady pull up the steep road ahead. Keep right at two junctions and out onto open moorland, where distant views of Whitby greet you.

Continue along the quiet road to reach a car park area, and a footpath sign on the left which points the way along a clear path for **Littlebeck**.

Cross a stile, and the busy A169, to follow it north on a wide verge. A gate on the right leads onto a track heading east, descending into the valley to join a broader track that leads down to Little Beck Lane.

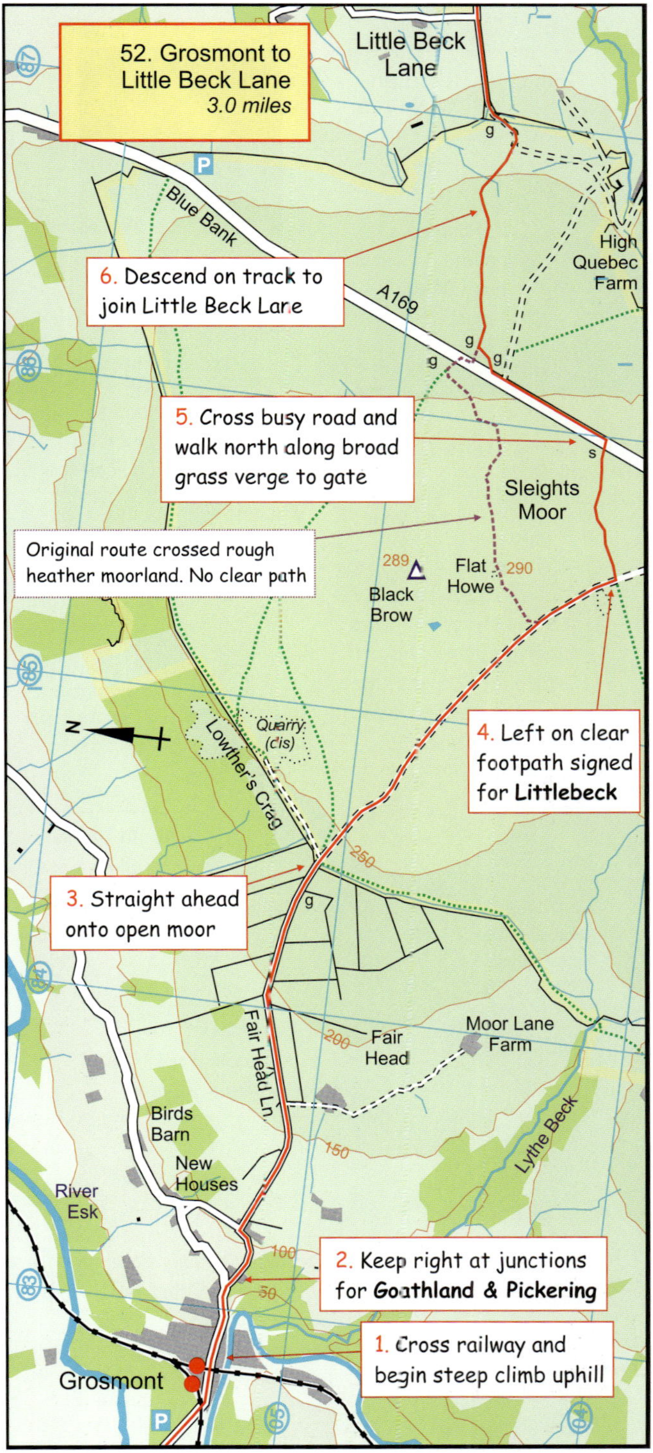

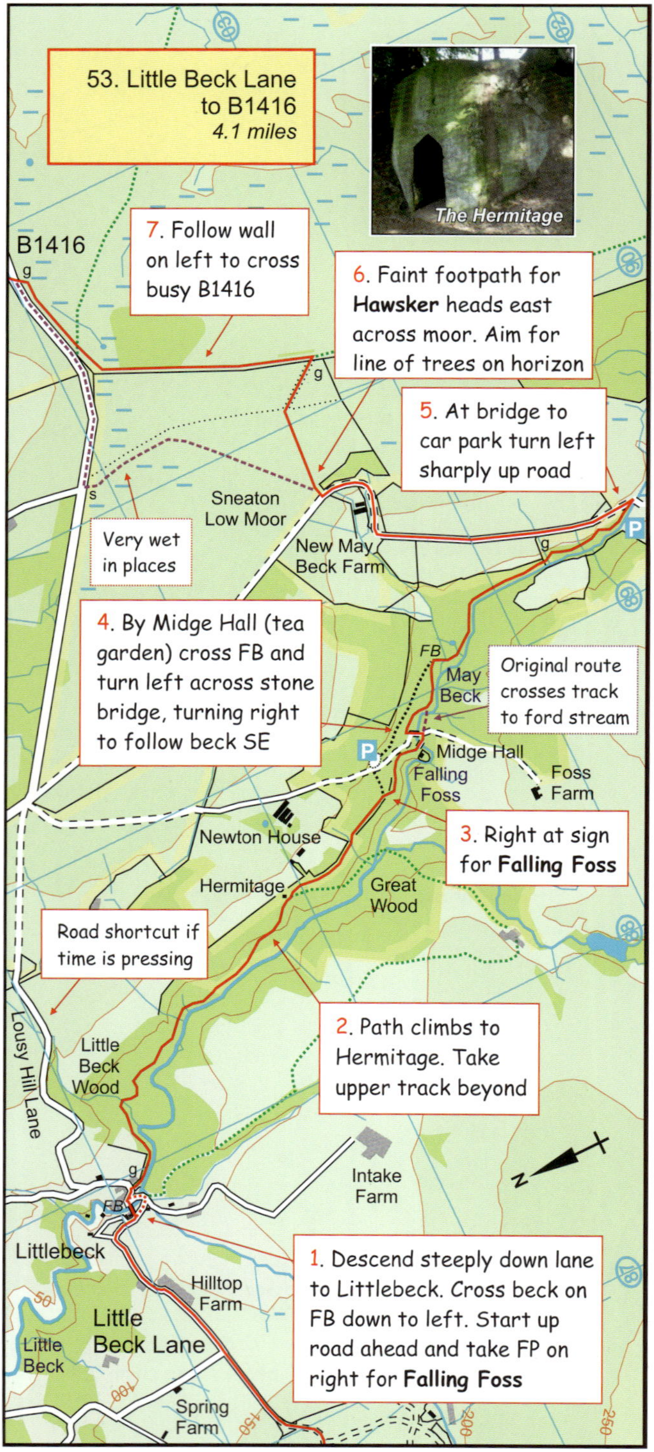

Pass through Littlebeck, crossing the beck at the footbridge, and as you begin to climb up the road, take a gate on the right into Little Beck Wood for **Falling Foss**. A delightful two-mile woodland walk now follows, above the eastern bank of Little Beck. The path climbs past the Hermitage, hewn from a single boulder by George Chubb in 1790, before descending again to Falling Foss and Midge Hall. It continues alongside May Beck, leading out eventually to the road at May Beck car park. Follow the road, sharp left, to pass New May Beck Farm. A faint footpath leads due east across Sneaton Low Moor to a wall gate at the end of a tree line. The wall leads to the B1416. Cross and join a clear footpath for **Hawsker** leading across the wet heather moorland of Graystone Hills.

The moor is left behind on a narrow, enclosed track, Stainsacre Lane. Turn right along the road to reach High Hawsker.

Continue up Robin Hood's Bay Road and at the sharp corner follow Bottoms Lane to Northcliffe Caravan Park. The way through is well signed, and soon you drop down to rejoin the Cleveland Way for the final three miles to Robin Hood's Bay. No problem route finding now. An exhilarating clifftop walk follows before finally, passing Ness Point, journey's end comes into view.

Make your way beyond the roundabout onto New Road, which leads steeply down, through tall clusters of red-roofed houses, into the heart of the fishing village. Step out onto the slipway, dip your boots in the North Sea, then head for the Bay Hotel and a well-earned pint or two.

Journey's end - dip your boots

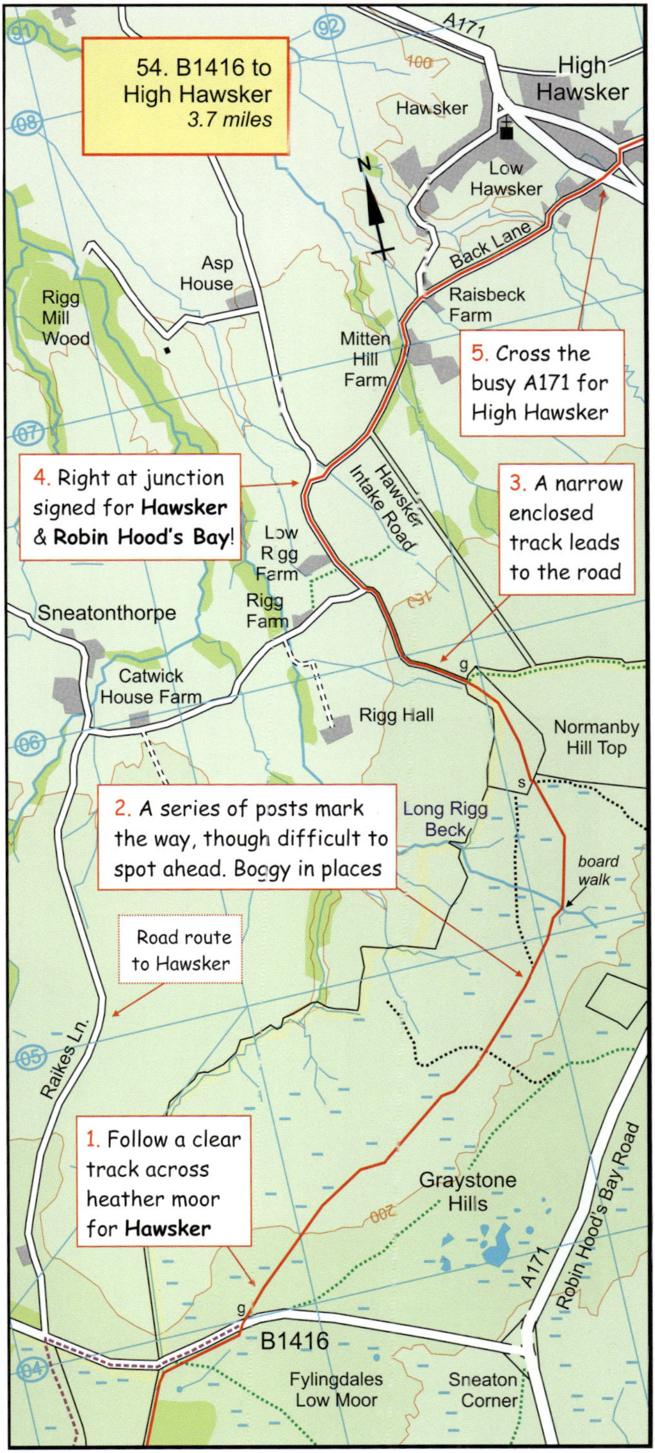

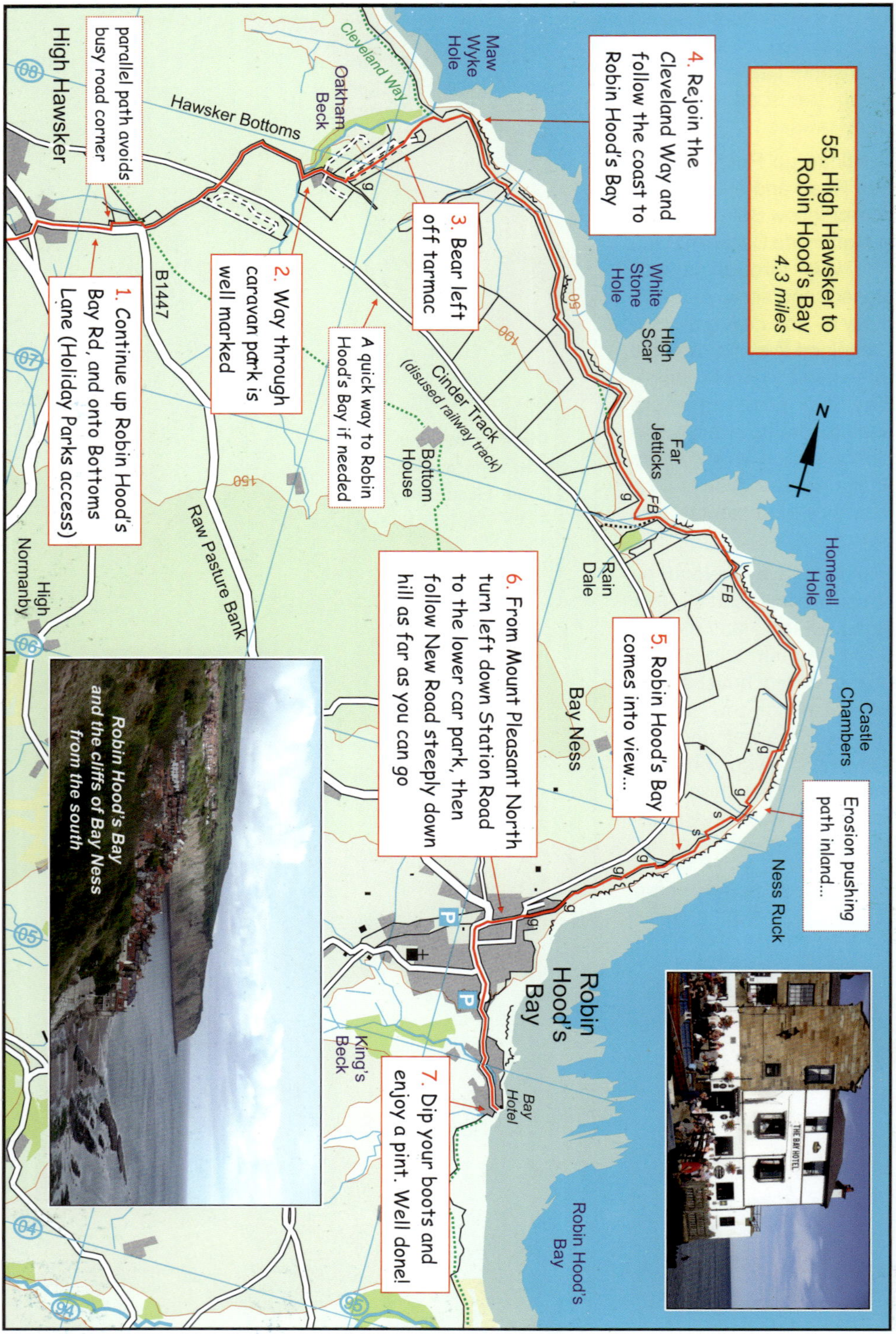
55. High Hawsker to Robin Hood's Bay
4.3 miles
1. Continue up Robin Hood's Bay Rd, and onto Bottoms Lane (Holiday Parks access)
2. Way through caravan park is well marked
3. Bear left off tarmac
4. Rejoin the Cleveland Way and follow the coast to Robin Hood's Bay
5. Robin Hood's Bay comes into view...
6. From Mount Pleasant North turn left down Station Road to the lower car park, then follow New Road steeply down hill as far as you can go
7. Dip your boots and enjoy a pint. Well done!
parallel path avoids busy road corner
A quick way to Robin Hood's Bay if needed
Erosion pushing path inland...
High Hawsker
High Normanby
Hawsker Bottoms
Oakham Beck
Cleveland Way
Maw Wyke Hole
White Stone Hole
High Scar
Far Jetticks
Homerell Hole
Castle Chambers
Ness Ruck
Rain Dale
Bay Ness
Bottom House
Cinder Track (disused railway track)
Raw Pasture Bank
B1447
Robin Hood's Bay
Bay Hotel
King's Beck
THE BAY HOTEL
Robin Hood's Bay and the cliffs of Bay Ness from the south